THE ART OF
Dream
Interpretation

THE ART OF
Dream
Interpretation

A practical guide to understanding your unconscious

BY LONA EVERSDEN

STERLING ETHOS
New York

STERLING ETHOS
New York

An Imprint of Sterling Publishing Co., Inc.
1166 Avenue of the Americas
New York, NY 10036

© 2017 Quarto Publishing Plc
Produced in 2017 by Quantum Books, an imprint of the Quarto Group.

ISBN 978-1-4549-2582-8

For information about custom editions, special sales, and premium
and corporate purchases, please contact Sterling Special Sales
at 800-805-5489 or specialsales@sterlingpublishing.com.

10 9 8 7 6 5 4 3 2 1

www.sterlingpublishing.com

Manufactured in China

CONTENTS

INTRODUCTION

We all dream—and in our dreams we enter a different world. This world may be peopled by family and friends, but also by fabulous creatures or superheroes. It can encompass the sidewalks and byways of home, as well as fantastical landscapes and impossible scenes.

Our dreams may seem inexplicable to us, but humankind has always known that the dream world has something to teach us about our lives and goals. Modern science hasn't yet revealed the full significance of dreaming, but we know that dreams can show the workings of our minds, and thus give us insights into our innermost desires and fears. This includes the feelings that we repress or deny knowledge of in our waking lives. Psychologists believe that our dreams can prompt memories, help us to process difficult or complex emotions, and serve as a kind of covert mental preparation for the challenges that we sense are in the offing.

READING THE DREAM

Learning to delve into the unconscious through your dreams can offer new insight into your motivations and ambitions; and can unlock a deeper understanding of the way you sometimes hinder your own development. Paying attention to your dreams can help you to know yourself better.

Dreams are products of our unconscious mind. They are a doorway into a part of ourselves that is normally hidden from us. The unconscious speaks to us in pictures, using whatever imagery is to hand. It takes our own long-held memories, the events of the day, our mental images of places and objects that we know and love or hate, and weaves them into a narrative that may well contain a useful message, something we should pay heed to. Everybody's mental furniture is different—no-one has exactly the same dreams as anyone else—but many themes and symbols are universal: The sun as an image of energy and power, a road as a metaphor for life's journey.

SPOTTING THE SYMBOLS

This book teaches you how to interpret your dreams and explains what the most common themes and symbols mean. But more than that, the perceptive text helps you to ask the pertinent questions that will lead to you to understand your own individual dream symbols. As you become familiar with the language of your dreams, you might notice that recurring or troubling dreams fade away, because you have received their message and understood it. Your dream life can become a fascinating journey in its own right.

▶ Called "The Interpreter," this 1811 colored etching shows a winged figure pointing to the dreamscape of a sleeping woman.

PART 1

THE WORLD OF DREAMS

Dreams are glimpses into the rich world that the unconscious mind creates for us while we sleep. Throughout history, humans have strived to interpret the meaning of these nighttime messages from our subliminal thoughts. This section briefly outlines the history of dream analysis, and provides practical tips on nurturing and developing your dreaming.

A BRIEF HISTORY OF DREAMING

Throughout history, humans have wondered about the meanings of their dreams. At first our ancestors looked to their dreams as they did to the stars—hoping to find guidance from their gods or intimations of the future. In modern times, with the birth of the science of psychology, we have gained new insights into the function of dreams. But dreaming remains a mysterious phenomenon: There is still a great deal that we do not understand.

THE ANCIENT EGYPTIANS

We know that the Egyptians were interested in the nature of dreams, because written fragments have come down to us. These fragments, known as the *Chester Beatty Papyrus III*, were written by a priest around 1220 B.C.E. They list interpretations of positive and negative dreams—in the sense they are good or bad omens. To dream of looking out of a window, for example, suggests your voice will be heard, while dreaming that your bed is on fire indicates that you are driving your spouse away.

ROMAN WISDOM

One of the great ancient studies of dreaming was carried out by a Roman scholar named Artemidorus, who lived in the second century C.E. In his work *Oneirocritica* (The Interpretation of Dreams), which spans five volumes, he made an attempt to classify dreams into various types (about the self, about public affairs, about the natural world, and so on). He offered interpretations of individual symbols in the manner of a dictionary. Like most ancients, Artemidorus believed that dreams foretold the future—but he also happened on some insights that seem to prefigure the work of Sigmund Freud.

For instance, he noticed that dreams can sometimes contain visual or verbal puns that can serve as clues to their meaning.

THE CHRISTIAN VIEW

For most of the past 2,000 years, Christians have believed that dreams are one of the ways in which God communicates with his people. Dreams are an important part of many biblical stories: In the Old Testament, Jacob dreamed of a ladder ascending to heaven; his son Joseph dreamed that he would rule over his older brothers—and so it transpired when he became vizier of Egypt; the prophet Daniel was an interpreter of dreams; and the New Testament Joseph, earthly father of Jesus, was visited by messenger angels in his dreams.

THE BIRTH OF PSYCHOANALYSIS

The idea that dreams were messages from God was overturned last century by Sigmund Freud (1856–1939), an Austrian neurologist and the founder of psychoanalysis. Freud understood that the unconscious mind was in constant conversation with the waking consciousness, and saw that dreams were the main channel of communication. He called dreams the "royal road to the

Unconscious"—meaning that analyzing dream stories was the best way to understand the suppressed desires that we explore in our sleep.

Freud's follower and successor, the psychologist Carl Jung (1875–1961), came to believe that Freud's view was too dark. Yes, dreams are sometimes expressions of wishes that are taboo or too shameful to be countenanced by the conscious mind, but generally the function of dreams is positive and creative: It is to reveal us to ourselves. Dreams do this in a symbolic language that is not confined to dreams alone. The same imagery finds expression throughout human culture—in fairy tales, myths, folk stories, paintings, plots of books, and even in movies. These cultural products are full of symbols—wise old men, temptresses, faithful sidekicks, epic journeys, and triumphant homecomings. These things are universal, and universally understood. Jung called these common symbols "archetypes." Once we learn to recognize and understand these symbols, we hold a powerful tool for decoding our own dreams.

A BRIEF HISTORY OF DREAMING

INTERPRETING YOUR DREAMS

Most of us have a natural fascination with our dreams. They are a bridge between our unconscious and conscious mind. They hint at our innermost fears and concerns, and so can provide us with deeper self-knowledge and encourage awareness. They are, in other words, a symbolic language in which the sleeping, unconscious part of us speaks to the wakeful, conscious self.

Dreams are best understood in the context of your own life: Certain symbols—even some of the most common ones—are bound to have a particular significance for you personally. So if you dream of, say, Paris or giraffes, ask yourself what comes to mind when you think of Paris or giraffes.

When you are trying to decode a dream, think about the setting and characters involved as well as the general events. What seems most significant? Is there anything odd or jarring? Try asking yourself the following questions:

1. What was the mood of the dream? What did I feel, in the dream itself and on awakening?
2. Where was I? What was the setting? Was there a sense of time—day or night, a particular hour?
3. What events occurred? Did the dream have a narrative, or was it a fragment?
4. Who was I in the dream? We do not always appear as ourselves, or we may be an observer rather than a participant.
5. Who else appeared in the dream? What do these people represent to me?
6. How did I feel in the dream—was I, for example, scared when I really shouldn't

have been, or entirely calm in a situation that would be terrifying in waking life. Such incongruities are clues.

THE SYMBOLS OF DREAMS

Our dreams are a way of processing emotions and thoughts, but they don't do this in a straightforward way. The mind uses imagery—sometimes surprising, always apt—to represent our hidden thought processes. The mind can also compress a range of events, themes, characters, and ideas into one symbol (Freud called this "condensation"), and it may transform an uncomfortable feeling or situation into something more acceptable to ourselves (what Freud called "displacement"). Metaphors, similes, and puns are all ways of signposting information or feelings.

Names Pay particular attention to any names you hear in your dreams. For example, if you suddenly dream of a long-forgotten geography teacher named Mrs. Keen—bear in mind that to keen is to weep with grief. It doesn't matter if you think you didn't know that—the unconscious mind knows many things that the conscious mind is unaware of.

Homonyms and Homophones Consider the idea that your unconscious mind likes wordplay. For example, if you find yourself in a fencing competition, then consider the fencing—the emotional barriers—that may be present in your life.

Metaphors and Similes The unconscious mind uses all the devices that we find in art and literature. Metaphor is one: In a dream, as in a poem or a picture, a dawn might stand for a new beginning, a crown

for power. And dreams are full of similes: If you or someone else appears in the form of a pig, then that might betoken greed or dirtiness; snow might stand for coldness—perhaps an emotionally chilly relationship.

CONSIDER THE OBVIOUS

Some dreams are simple reminders. Dreaming of a certain friend or relative may be a sign that you feel bad for neglecting him or her and know that it is time to call or meet. If a leg features prominently in your dream, that might make you aware of a nagging knee pain that you have been ignoring and prompt you to get it checked out.

INTERPRETING YOUR DREAMS

NURTURING YOUR DREAM LIFE

If you want to nurture your dream life, then it is important to prioritize having a good night's sleep; we need long periods of uninterrupted sleep in order to dream—and also to stay healthy. When you get into bed, take a few moments to breathe deeply and relax. Tell yourself you are looking forward to your dreams and all they can tell you.

You can use the power of autosuggestion to encourage particular dreams: Try saying "I love my dreams. Tonight I am going to dream about flying," and see what happens.

TIPS FOR SLEEP

For good sleep, it is helpful to go to bed and to wake up at the same time each day. Before you go to bed, spend a few minutes consciously relaxing, perhaps by having a warm bath or doing some gentle stretches. Avoid alcohol before bed (it can affect the quality of your dreams as well as that of your sleep), as well as caffeinated drinks in the afternoon. Don't eat a heavy meal within three hours of bedtime. Use soft lighting, which encourages the body to relax in preparation for sleep, and avoid activities such as watching TV or looking at a smartphone, since screens emit a blue light that disrupts sleep. Make sure your bedroom is a comfortable place that encourages sleep by making it dark enough, clean, and free from clutter.

IMPROVING RECALL

When you wake, don't leap straight out of bed. Take a few moments to write down your dream in a journal (see pages 16–17).

This is the key step in encouraging better recall, and also aids with interpretation. If you do not remember anything, then simply write about the way you are feeling; this may prompt a memory of the dream, and in time can encourage better recall.

It is usually easier to remember your dreams if you wake up naturally rather than being shocked into wakefulness by an alarm clock. If you do need to use an alarm, try one that uses soft music or turn down the volume.

You can encourage yourself to remember your dreams by using a short affirmative phrase, such as "I find it easy to remember my dreams." Say this to yourself before you drift into sleep and at random intervals during the day.

EXERCISE YOUR AWARENESS

Another way to become more aware of your dreams and the symbols that occur in them, is to work on becoming more aware in your waking life. Observe one situation or object in detail each day. Sit on a park bench and spend a few minutes noticing the colors, textures, sounds, and aromas around you. Notice the pathway,

▲ Sleep is an essential part of healing the body and dreaming allows us to process events and emotions. To help facilitate this, make your bedroom a restful place to be.

the trees and plants, any people who are nearby. Then take out a notebook and pen and write down or sketch the scene in as much detail as possible before looking up at it again. This is a good way to train your eye and your powers of recall.

LUCID DREAMING

In lucid dreaming, the dreamer remains aware that he or she is dreaming, and is able to direct the events of the dream. So you might choose to fly, to recall an old friend and chat with them, or to be a skillful acrobat. Lucid dreaming is a form of spiritual practice in Tibetan Buddhism and Hindu tantric traditions, but practitioners say that anyone can train themselves to do it, using deep relaxation techniques, visualization, and affirmations. Try telling yourself "I will remain aware in my dreams tonight" before you fall asleep. If you wake up after a dream, you can try visualizing the same scene to lull yourself back to sleep.

KEEPING A DREAM JOURNAL

The best way to remember your dreams and develop your skills of interpretation is to keep a dream journal. Try to have this to hand, together with a pen, so that you can record your dreams as soon as you wake up—it's also worth having a torch within reach, in case you want to write down a dream without putting on a bright light or disturbing your partner.

A journal is a very personal object and you should choose it thoughtfully. You may like to have a small lined notepad, or loose paper in a binder; if you like to draw scenes from your dreams as well as write notes, then a larger artist's sketchpad may suit you better. Some people like to record their dreams on a computer or phone, but this is less evocative than putting pen to paper. You may find it helpful to use a Dictaphone, then transcribe the dream later.

ORGANIZING YOUR JOURNAL

Use one page of the book for writing the details of your dream and the opposite page for making notes about your interpretation (or draw a rule down the center of the page, if you prefer). Always write the date at the top of the page—it may have symbolic relevance and can also help you keep track of how often a particular image or scene recurs. Keep a few pages at the back of the journal for jotting down recurring images and characters—these can provide fascinating insights into your principle motivations and fears.

WRITING DOWN YOUR DREAMS

Try to record the prevailing emotion of the dream—fear, pleasure, anger—as well as your mood on waking. Sometimes an apparently angry dream may leave you feel happy or relieved when you wake up, a dissonance that may be significant. If there was a particular color associated with the dream, make a note of that too.

It is important to write up your dreams as soon as you wake—even the most vivid dreams fade very quickly. Note as much detail as you can. Try to record the dream just as it occurred, in the same order of events, and without trying to interpret it as you go along. Avoid any temptation to leave out particular scenes or symbols, and make sure you include the setting, any characters who appeared, or any names that you remember. Give the dream a title if one comes to mind. If you can't remember much about the dream, just record what you do recollect—the very process of writing your dream down may prompt your memory.

YOUR INTERPRETATION PAGE

Jot down a few notes about what you think the dream meant. Don't think too hard about this. Then try underlining any keywords and symbols in your account of the dream. Go through these, examining

▲ Keeping a journal provides you with a fascinating record of your dreams, and the very act of writing helps to stimulate your powers of recall.

what each one means to you, and consider them together too—a ball and a chain in a dream could point to the old phrase about marriage. Think about whether the symbols or names could be a pun. A green mist might be a symbol for a Mr. Green. Look up the symbols in the directory in this book and read each entry. Does this spark new lines of inquiry for you?

Don't worry if you cannot interpret your dream straight away, it may be that things become clear later when you re-read a journal entry in the context of other dreams, or in relation to subsequent events in your life. Dreams are much like a story that you read in installments: Some things inevitably remain unresolved until a chapter or two later.

PART 2

DIRECTORY OF SYMBOLS

Our unconscious uses visual imagery to communicate with us in dreams, drawing on the universal symbolism we are instinctively familiar with. Organized thematically, this directory introduces the most common dream motifs that we encounter, explaining their key associations in various cultures and providing guidelines for interpretation of the symbols within a dream scenario.

HOW TO USE THE DIRECTORY

This directory is organized into general themes to allow you to explore the meanings of associated ideas and symbols easily. The themes relate to the key areas of our lives, from the human body to natural landscapes, and from everyday items to people and places.

You should treat this directory as a starting point for your own exploration into the enigma of your dreams or fragments of dreams. The insightful text will show you the multiple meanings associated with the common symbols that recur in our dreams, using examples from mythology and different cultures across the world, which can permeate our unconscious minds. It also draws on the work of some of the great dream analysts, such as Sigmund Freud and Carl Jung.

Because all of us have a very personal history, we can have very different associations with everyday objects, roles, and landscapes. Your feelings about a police officer might be very different if your partner is one, than if you were once arrested, for example. The mind is adept at integrating these personal associations with the universal symbolism that we all tap into, and using it to convey a message. For this reason, you should always consider your own history and feelings toward a symbol as well as its general description.

Your feelings in the dream are also an important aspect of your decoding. If you react with horror to something that is seemingly benign, or embrace something that is usually monstrous, that can tell you something about whether your unconscious mind is giving you a warning or urging you to clear an obstacle and move forward.

DREAM THEMES

A visual representation of the theme from art, popular culture, or everyday life.

WASHING

▲ This painting shows a monk washing the feet of Christ, an act of humility.

An overview of the general topic, exploring its functions or significance in our waking lives, any mythological meanings, and its symbolism in our dreams.

The act of washing is about more than hygiene—it is a ritual activity in many cultures, signifying new beginnings and a change in the mindset (usually before worship). Since water denotes the emotions and the unconscious, it matters what the water is like in the dream: Is it clean or murky? And is there anything in the water? Where you are washing may also be significant. If it is in a place that you recognize, what associations do you have with that place?

The most positive and joyful messages that the symbol may carry. Even an apparently unhappy symbol, such as funeral, can carry a message of hope.

POSITIVE INTERPRETATION
Cleaning is usually a positive act of purification, and may suggest some radical change of heart or direction, or perhaps a desire to be forgiven. Washing in a bathroom or other private space could be related to self-nurture, while washing other people suggests caring for them or dealing with difficulties in your relationships.

NEGATIVE INTERPRETATION
Washing or bathing in dirty water suggests you feel unable to resolve some muddy issue. Think about the pun potential of what you are cleaning in the dream and if wordplay could shed more light on the deeper meaning of the dream.

WASHING THE FEET
Washing someone else's feet is an act of devotion and humility in many religions. Whose feet are you washing, or is it your feet that are being washed?

WASHING THE HANDS
This act is associated with freeing oneself of guilt, or it may be a visual reference to the idea of washing your hands of a situation—in the sense of denying responsibility of it.

DOING THE LAUNDRY
Laundry could be a metaphor for personal or family affairs; dirty laundry suggests that something needs attending to. The saying "washing one's dirty linen in public" could be significant—has private information about you been exposed? The type of dirt or stains on the laundry may help to pinpoint the meaning of the dream. A washing machine in a dream may indicate some kind of emotional turbulence, or a cycle of events.

Pithy descriptions of the meaning of deeper or alternate aspects of the topic or symbols that are related to it.

The darker meanings of the symbol, especially when it appears in a nightmare or unpleasant dream.

THE LIFE & AGE
OF WOMAN.

STAGES OF WOMAN'S LIFE
FROM THE
CRADLE TO THE GRAVE.

Entered according to Act of Congress in the Year 1848, by J. Baillie, in the Clerks Office of the Dist. Court of the South Dist. of N.Y.

Published by James Baillie, 87th St. near 3rd Avenue N.Y.

Stages of Life

PREGNANCY

▲ Hormonal changes mean women often dream more vividly during pregnancy.

A pregnancy dream in a woman of childbearing age may be a wish-fulfillment dream, reflecting a literal desire to have a baby. Sometimes a woman who is trying to conceive may dream she has been successful before finding out that is indeed the case (the unconscious mind may pick up on changes in the body). More commonly, though, a pregnancy dream is symbolic and often indicates that you may be about to "give birth" to a new idea or project. Pregnancy dreams are more common among women than men, but men can also have them (a pregnant woman may represent the feminine or creative side of a male dreamer).

POSITIVE INTERPRETATION

Pregnancy dreams are usually positive. Since pregnancy is concerned with an act of creation, it can indicate that you are about to embark on a new, more creative phase of your life or a period of personal growth.

NEGATIVE INTERPRETATION

A woman who fears getting pregnant or giving birth may have an unpleasant pregnancy dream. It is common to dream of giving birth to a monster during a real-life pregnancy—a reflection of the normal anxieties that many mothers-to-be experience.

GIVING BIRTH

A difficult labor suggests hard work is needed to realize a current project. Having an assisted birth (such as a Caesarian section) suggests you need help from another person. Dreaming you are a midwife or birthing partner shows that you have the ability to "birth" a plan or idea.

INFERTILITY

If this dream does not indicate actual fears or feelings about infertility, it could mean that you do not have an outlet for your creativity or that you feel lacking in creative ideas.

MISCARRIAGE OR STILLBIRTH

This scenario may suggest that a promising idea no longer seems viable, or is perhaps a sign that you need an alternative path of action. Dreaming that someone else has a miscarriage or stillbirth can indicate that your association has become fruitless.

◀ This hand-colored lithograph from the 1840s shows the stages of life from cradle to grave, which are a rich source of material for our dreamscapes.

BABIES

▲ A baby can represent a longing to be nourished and nurtured.

Like pregnancy dreams, baby dreams are often about creativity and hope. But a baby can also represent the most innocent and purest part of yourself, or an aspect of your personality or a talent that is immature and needs nurturing. A dream of a baby may reflect feelings of helplessness or a wish to return to a time when you were cared for and had no responsibilities. Key to interpretation are your feelings about the baby in the dream and whether it is thriving. The dream can also reflect an active wish to have a baby or a fear of parenthood.

POSITIVE INTERPRETATION

If the baby in the dream is happy and well cared for, this suggests you feel positive about life or about a new project or idea that you are nurturing. This is a time that is full of potential, hope, and new beginnings.

NEGATIVE INTERPRETATION

Is the baby neglected or crying? If so, you may be feeling starved of affection or some kind of sustenance. Perhaps you are ignoring your potential, or need physical or spiritual comfort. Alternatively this dream could reflect worries that you are not providing for a child or dependent in real life.

SOMEONE ELSE'S BABY

If you are given another person's baby to care for in your dream, then this suggests someone has burdened you with unwelcome responsibilities.

A DYING BABY

This dream symbol can suggest we feel an inability to provide for some deep need within ourselves or another person. It can also signal the symbolic death of some aspect of ourselves that we need to come to terms with.

AN UMBILICAL CORD

If the baby still has the umbilical cord attached to it, this can indicate a dependent relationship with another person—to whom the cord has not been cut. Cutting the cord, conversely, signals greater independence.

BAPTISM AND INITIATION

▲ Baptism signals some kind of rebirth, and a cleansing or purification.

The Christian ritual of baptism involves the symbolic washing away of sin and a return to a pure state. A dream involving this therefore suggests that there is a past event or difficulty that you wish to cleanse away, so that you can emerge anew. But a body of water is often a picture of the unconscious itself—so a dream of immersion implies that you are beginning to explore those depths. Anointing with water (or oil) may suggest a sense of being chosen or a desire to be chosen.

POSITIVE INTERPRETATION

A dream of baptism can signal a change of attitude or circumstances that allow one to embrace new possibilities in life. It often means that one stage of your life has ended and that you are about to begin a new one. Baptism dreams may also take the form of undergoing some kind of ordeal (as in "baptism of fire"). In such dreams, the outcome is key.

NEGATIVE INTERPRETATION

Resistance to a baptism shows a resistance to inner change, or a feeling that you are paying lip-service to certain customs in order to gain your place in a group.

A BLESSING

Receiving a religious blessing of some sort shows a need for approval, or perhaps reveals an inner conviction that one is doing the right thing.

INITIATION

Any form of initiation ceremony suggests that you are on the threshold of some form of acceptance, by yourself or within a wider group or community. An initiation dream may occur if you are about to take on a new role, which requires one to take on a new identity.

COMING OF AGE

In an older person, dreaming of a past ritual such as a school prom or a graduation can signal regret that opportunities have been missed or are now past.

FOUR SYMBOLS

A Christian baptism rite involves water, candles, oil, and white robes, so the appearance of these symbols can indicate a baptism dream even if the ritual is not taking place. If you are from or connected to a different tradition, then be on the lookout for the relevant symbols.

STAGES OF LIFE

BIRTHDAYS

▲ Blowing out candles may suggest the end of a phase. How many are there?

Ceremonies of all kinds are generally positive and joyful dreams. Birthdays are a way of celebrating the uniqueness of an individual, and may indicate that you have something to celebrate in real life. And they represent affirmation, since others share the fun with you. Birthdays also mark the passage of time, so this can suggest optimism about the future or, conversely, a fear that time is passing too quickly, depending on your feelings in the dream. More prosaically, a birthday dream may be your mental calendar reminding you of an important appointment or anniversary that is coming up.

POSITIVE INTERPRETATION

A joyful birthday party in which you are dancing or celebrating with guests is an indication that you feel good about yourself and recognized and loved by others. It can suggest good fortune has come your way (or you think it is about to), or may indicate the birth of a new stage of your life. Being included in another person's birthday suggests that you feel positively about this person or are hoping to share in his or her success.

NEGATIVE INTERPRETATION

Having your birthday forgotten or marred in some way suggests that you are craving affection or recognition from others and feel overlooked.

A GIFT

A present from someone can highlight how you feel about your relationship with him or her. If it remains unwrapped, it may be someone you have difficulty accepting. Giving someone else a present expresses a wish to be accepted. Puns are common in dreams: Is this a comment on the "present" moment?

A BIRTHDAY CAKE

This signifies generosity, a desire or ability to share what you have with other people.

CANDLES

Candles are ancient symbols with many associations: hope, potential, enlightenment, fragility. The exact number of candles may have some significance for the dreamer. Blowing candles out represents an ending of some sort in your life. (*See Lights, Candles, and Torches, page 95.*)

WEDDINGS

▲ A happy wedding dream can be a symbol of integration and partnership.

This can be a wish-fulfillment dream, especially if you are single in real life. If you are married, then it may suggest that you are reaffirming your commitment to your spouse, or perhaps thinking about your relationship and what it means. Historically, weddings were the union of a man and a woman, and so a wedding can represent the healthy integration of the masculine and feminine sides of yourself. Or it can be the coming-together of ideas, plans, and hopes. (*See Rings, page 87.*)

POSITIVE INTERPRETATION

Wedding dreams are usually happy dreams, signaling a new beginning or a long-term commitment to a person or a project. Who you are getting married to is significant. If it is an older man or woman, this could signify your need for security or a parental figure. If you are watching someone else get married, then they may represent your own feelings about matrimony. The tradition in which you are getting married may reveal something about the culture this comes from if it is not your own.

NEGATIVE INTERPRETATION

A wedding in which you feel unhappy probably reflects concerns that you have about a commitment in your waking life. A forced marriage, running away from the ceremony, or having difficulty making your way to a wedding all suggest that you are not ready to embrace a change of direction or make an important decision.

BRIDESMAIDS

Being a bridesmaid could signal that you are in a new romance, or wish to get married. The phrase "always a bridesmaid, never a bride" could be significant: Do you feel that opportunities have been missed?

WEDDING ANNIVERSARIES

Dreaming of an anniversary could be an acknowledgment of the importance of love in your life (or, sometimes, simply a useful reminder that an important date is coming up).

WHITE WEDDINGS

A white dress symbolizes purity in the West and may represent your moral judgments about behavior. The wedding dress is an outward expression of a commitment being made, but if you are wearing one in an unusual situation (such as at work), it can suggest feelings of unworthiness. Veils can symbolize hiding an aspect of yourself.

DEATH

▲ A skull represents mortality, or a need to expose what is going on in the mind.

A death in a dream—like the figure of Death in the tarot—is always symbolic: Dreamed deaths never foretell the death of the dreamer or anyone else. A death in a dream is usually a metaphor for a significant ending—perhaps irrevocable, usually positive. Look carefully at who has died in the dream and under what circumstances, and explore those associations: There will be clues to the deeper meaning.

POSITIVE INTERPRETATION

You can see a death dream as a signal that you are acknowledging the end of one stage of your life, whether this is chosen or forced upon you, or perhaps an outdated habit or personal characteristic. A death dream can herald acceptance, and so mark the beginning of a rebirth or a new episode in your life.

NEGATIVE INTERPRETATION

Dreaming that someone else is dead can reflect a subconscious desire to remove that person from your life, or that you need to remove some characteristic that person represents from your own psyche. Having a corpse in your dream can suggest that you are trying pointlessly to maintain something that has already died, clinging to a hope that no longer exists.

DEATH OF A CHILD

This dream scenario can signify the loss of innocence or an acceptance that adulthood can involve the sacrifice of carefree or childlike habits and pleasure.

DEATH CERTIFICATE

This can be a reminder that life is short and that you need to make time for the things that are most important to you, or it may be alerting you to an important deadline for which time is running out.

DREAMING OF A DECEASED PERSON

It's very common to dream of those who have died, and this is a way of maintaining your connection to them or reflecting on their significance in your life (for good or ill). If you dream that you are communicating with someone who has died, this can suggest you feel there was more to be said. Such dreams can be a helpful way of working through feelings of loss.

FUNERALS AND BURIALS

▲ Funeral dreams can reflect a need to process an ending of some kind.

Funerals are often seen as a celebration of a person's life as well as a way of marking an ending, and so a funeral dream can feel positive. Often though, this is your psyche's way of facing up to a change or ending in your life—something is dead and buried and needs to be laid to rest. How you feel about this change will be reflected by your feelings in the dream. It will also be significant to note whose funeral it is.

POSITIVE INTERPRETATION

Perhaps a relationship has ended or you have left a job; this dream is reassurance that you are ready to let go of one phase of your life—leaving the past behind—and embrace the changes that are taking place. A large gathering at your own funeral may reflect positive feelings about what you have achieved so far in life, and a sense that others appreciate you.

NEGATIVE INTERPRETATION

Sometimes a funeral dream may reflect in a literal way your anxieties about the health of the person who is being buried. Or a funeral about another person can be a desire to remove him or her from your life, or to be more independent of this person (this is especially true if you are dreaming about the funeral of a parent). If your partner is the person being buried, then this may reflect feelings of sadness or isolation within the relationship, or a more general feeling of loneliness and lack of support in your life.

COFFINS

If you are in the coffin and cannot get out, this can suggest feeling trapped in a situation. Otherwise, a coffin represents your feelings about your own mortality or acceptance of a change in your life. A coffin of someone else may reflect a desire to get rid of him or her, or alternatively a fear of losing this person from your life. If the person is already dead, then this probably represents the influence they had on your life.

UNDERTAKERS

An undertaker is someone who prepares the dead for burial, but one also undertakes to do an important task. Thus the appearance of an undertaker can either represent an obligation to take on responsibility, or your feelings about someone who is undertaking something for you.

A HEARSE OR PROCESSION

A funeral procession is a slow-moving thing, and so dreaming of a hearse could simply be presenting an image of lack of progress. (*See Cars, pages 78–79.*)

STAGES OF LIFE

KILLING AND VIOLENT DEATH

Dreams often exaggerate the feelings or emotions that we experience in daily life. According to one German study, people who often dream about killing other people may be aggressive in the waking hours and may also be more introverted. Other psychologists disagree and argue that dreaming of killing another person is much more likely to be symbolic, reflecting a desire to kill off a particular aspect of your own psyche—perhaps an undesirable habit or attitude.

POSITIVE INTERPRETATION

A killing dream may indicate that you have taken control and are trying to deal with an unpleasant or harmful behavior or character trait. It's important to consider whether you are the killer or the victim, as this can indicate your level of control or powerlessness.

NEGATIVE INTERPRETATION

Are you under a lot of pressure at the moment? Or feeling angry or bitter toward another person? A killing dream can reflect intense negative emotion that is being suppressed.

STRANGLING OR SUFFOCATION

Are you feeling smothered by somebody in your life? Or are you repressing some important emotion? If you are the one being choked, then this suggests that you are unable to express yourself.

DROWNING

Water symbolizes your emotional life *(see Water, page 110)*, and drowning can mean that you are feeling overwhelmed by your feelings and unable to keep your head above water. If you are at sea in the dream, then the issues may be too big for you to manage, while drowning in a swimming pool suggests that the issue is more contained. Saving someone from drowning indicates that you have confidence in your ability to rescue the situation. Sometimes a drowning dream could suggest rebirth.

BURIED ALIVE

To dream of burial—especially of burial alive—is often an indication that the dreamer is delving into the unconscious (just like immersion in water). This can be scary, but in the end is always fruitful.

EXECUTION OR DEATH SENTENCE

Dreaming of an execution can be a sign that you have done something that you think is unforgivable or fear that others will deem it to be so. Alternatively, this dream can occur when you have a pressing deadline or an urgent need to do something before it is too late. Receiving a death sentence is a way of telling yourself that change is needed.

POISONING

This suggests that a negative attitude is proving toxic to your life and ambitions, or that another person is a harmful influence in your life and you need to cleanse yourself of him or her.

SHOOTING OR STABBING

Being shot or stabbed indicates you have suffered some wound to your feelings. Shooting someone else can mean you harbor violent feelings toward them. Since both a knife and gun can be a phallic symbol (a visual metaphor for the penis), this dream can also concern sexual feelings. *(See Weapons, page 91.)*

TORTURE

In waking life we often use the word "torture" to indicate mental anguish or difficulty, and this is what it represents in a dream. The type of torture and the part of the body affected may be significant.

▲ Violent dreams can be disturbing. They can symbolize a feeling that you are being treated badly, or that you yourself are an aggressor.

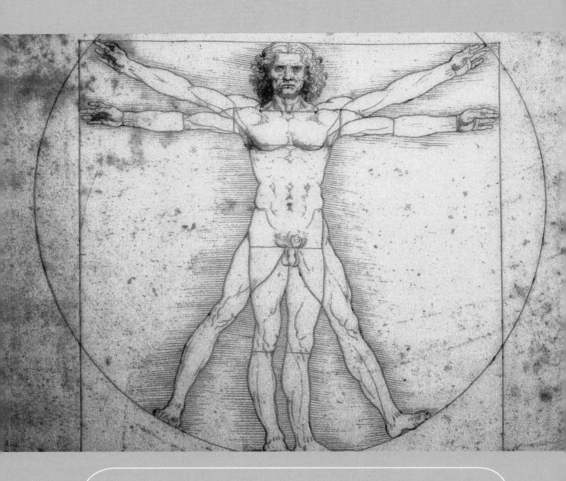

The Human Body

BREASTS

▲ The breasts can symbolize life, nurture, and abundance.

Breasts are powerful symbols in dreams. It is at our mother's breast that we first receive nurture, so the breast represents maternal care and also sustenance and generosity. It is a symbol of female sexuality, and so can represent sexual fulfillment or desire. There are several phrases containing the word "breasts" which may be relevant—"beating one's breast" with grief and admitting to a wrongdoing by "making a clean breast of it."

POSITIVE INTERPRETATION

Sustenance comes in many forms, and a positive dream about breasts may reflect a feeling of having enough in life. In a woman's dream, breasts may represent her feelings about motherhood or femininity, her willingness to care for and nurture others, or sexual pleasure. In a man's dream, they are more likely to reflect sexual desire.

NEGATIVE INTERPRETATION

A negative dream about breasts, or a dream of wrinkled or empty breasts, could be an allusion to a sense of not being sustained in life generally, or perhaps reflects a negative financial situation. A woman's dream could reflect a health concern here, or be a reminder to check the breasts.

◀ Body and mind are inextricably linked. Each part of the body relates to different aspects of the physical, emotional, and spiritual life.

PLACING ONE'S HEAD ON A BREAST

This dream suggests a weariness and dependence. Perhaps one wishes to return to the state of a being baby when all one's needs were taken care of?

BREASTFEEDING

Nourishing a baby shows a willingness to put time and energy into an idea or project, to nourish it and help it to grow. An unpleasant dream suggests you are giving too much, or something or someone is sucking the life out of you. If you are the one feeding, is your hunger being satisfied or not?

CHEST AND HEART

Our emotions are often felt in the chest or heart area, and so dreams about these parts of the body reflect emotions, especially love, pride, or vanity.

BUTTOCKS
AND THE BACK

▲ The back can represent a hidden side to us, or a wish to avoid something.

When the buttocks play a significant role in your dream, your unconscious could be suggesting that your baser instincts are driving your actions. The back has many possible interpretations depending on its context. It can indicate that something is happening that we are unaware of (on a conscious level), or that we have put a situation behind us. Are you backing off or turning your back on something or someone? Or do you need to watch your back, or want someone to provide back-up?

POSITIVE INTERPRETATION

The buttocks have sexual connotations, and a sensual dream concerning them could be one of wish fulfillment. Buttocks may also suggest division, a dichotomy, or a choice. A happy dream about the back could suggest an awareness of the support you have in your life or your body of friends.

NEGATIVE INTERPRETATION

Dreams of uncleanliness could represent discomfort or shame about your base instincts. A dream of pain in this area of the body could be a literal expression of you or someone else being a "pain in the butt." If your back is bent, then are you unable to stand up for yourself in your waking life? (*See Skeleton and Bones, page 45.*)

A STAB IN THE BACK

Do you feel betrayed by someone close to you, or fear that a rival is using underhand means to get ahead? Or are you the person doing the stabbing, and who are you harming?

A KICK IN THE BUTTOCKS

If you are being kicked in the butt in a dream then this could mean that you need to get on with something you have been delaying. Alternatively, it could be a sign that you feel bad about something you have done and believe you should be punished for it.

DEFECATION

This dream can reflect a desire to eliminate harmful emotions from your system, or sometimes self-disgust. Freud believed feces represented money, and a defecation dream can point you toward your feelings about wealth. (*See Bathrooms and Toilets, page 72.*)

LEGS AND FEET

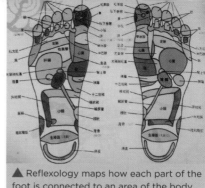

▲ Reflexology maps how each part of the foot is connected to an area of the body.

Our legs and feet root us to the ground, giving us stability and connecting us to the planet that gives us life. But they also carry us through life, so dreams about these parts of the body can be about movement and progress. Feet can represent spirituality, and going barefoot is a symbol of spirituality and spiritual seeking in many religious traditions.

POSITIVE INTERPRETATION

Healthy legs and feet are a sign that you have a good support system, and feel able to "stand on your own two feet." If you are walking, your pace and progress are an indication of the advancement you are making in your waking life. Consider how you feel about your walk and also your surroundings—all journeys happen in a landscape, after all—to see what they suggest to you.

NEGATIVE INTERPRETATION

Cold feet could suggest reluctance over a course of action that you are committed to—or it could suggest you feel unsupported in some way. Aching feet may signify that you cannot continue on your current course. A dream of amputation could mean that you need help from some external source—or, conversely, that there is something that you must let go of, however painful it seems.

KNEES

The knee often stands for a change that contains an element of continuity, since it both divides and joins the two parts of the leg. Knees can represent forebears and descendants—the word "knee" comes from the same ancient root as the words "gene" and "generation." It can also represent flexibility.

TOES

We have a subconscious memory of a time when our prehensile toes were as useful as our fingers in gripping trees, and toes can suggest unexplored or unused potential. We can be kept "on our toes" or made to "toe the line," so toes can be about discipline or restriction (which may be irksome or useful).

HEELS AND ANKLES

These can represent a weak spot—the Achilles heel in Greek myth is an area of vulnerability. Is this dream a warning?

ARMS AND HANDS

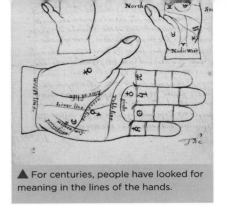

▲ For centuries, people have looked for meaning in the lines of the hands.

Our arms and hands allow us to hold and use tools, reach out, and connect with others. We also use them to defend ourselves—the word "arms" is a synonym for weapons. A dream in which these body parts feature prominently could signify how equipped you feel for whatever you are facing in your waking life. Hands symbolize our life as a whole, since our fortune is said to be imprinted on the folds and creases on our palms. Inspecting your hands in a dream can be a wish to better understand yourself or the past, or to know the future—as in chiromancy or palm reading.

POSITIVE INTERPRETATION

Dexterity in a dream can show that we are handling things well in our waking life. Since the hands are the principal means by which we feel things, they can be a metaphor for our emotions; holding hands can represent unity or commitment. We also use our arms to ward off an aggressor, so they may imply protection or the need to defend ourselves. The "coat of arms" is the term for a shield and also represents your family, which may be significant.

NEGATIVE INTERPRETATION

Dirty or bloody hands can be a sign of shame or guilt. A missing hand can suggest you feel unable to tackle a task, as can an injured or broken arm.

ELBOWS

A symbol of pushing ahead through difficulty. We elbow our way through a crowd, and also need to use "elbow grease" to tackle a stubborn task.

FINGERS

The index finger is used for pointing and could suggest a need to take a different direction, while the left ring finger can symbolize marriage or commitment. The middle finger is used to make an obscene gesture—is there someone that you wish to raise the finger to? The thumb is often a phallic symbol in dreams.

THE RIGHT AND LEFT HAND

Being left-handed was traditionally associated with bad luck or evil, so if the left hand is prominent in a dream this could be significant. In some cultures, the left hand is considered unclean and offering a left hand is an insult.

SKIN

▲ Tattoos have long been used as talismans for those facing battle.

At the most basic level, the skin demarcates where we begin; in the world of dreams it can represent our identity and the way we are seen by others. We talk of being comfortable in our own skin, jumping out of our skin, or of someone else getting under our skin. Since our skin forms the barrier between ourselves and the outside world, it has a defensive function—sometimes we need a thick skin to protect ourselves from outside hurts.

POSITIVE INTERPRETATION

If skin seems to be significant in your dream, think about its healthiness, age, and texture—glowing, smooth, young skin suggests you feel good about yourself. Bare skin can be a sign that you are ready for intimacy or to reveal yourself to another person. Sudden peeling of the skin can suggest that you are ready to "shed your skin" like a snake, and shrug off old attitudes or take on a new identity. (*See Being Naked, page 54.*)

NEGATIVE INTERPRETATION

Wounds or blemishes on the skin may indicate feelings of vulnerability, or emotional wounds that are not healing. Similarly, dreaming that the skin is deteriorating in some way can intimate that your defenses are being breached. A rash appearing on the skin could be a play on words: Are you making a rash decision?

TATTOOS

A tattoo is a permanent marker on our skin, something that we display to the world. In a dream, it might be a reference to a relationship or event that has left a permanent mark on you. It can also indicate belonging to a particular group, or may be a protective talisman. Consider the design, color, and position of the tattoo. Does it include any words?

WRINKLES

If your skin appears older in a dream, then this can be a straightforward fear about aging or indicate that something important to your sense of self has been spoiled. But with age comes experience, so wrinkles in a dream could also suggest you have become wiser in some way.

SCABS AND SCARS

Think about how you have reacted to these signs of old injuries in the dream. Are you picking at a scab, preventing an old injury from healing? A scar is the remnant and reminder of an injury; it could suggest that one has learned from a painful past experience, or needs to do so.

FACES

We recognize each other by our facial features, and so the face is a powerful symbol of our self-image in dreams. It may represent the image that we present to the outside world, or perhaps the image that we would like to present. The face can also be a barometer of our emotional state, as our emotions are reflected in our expression; are you putting a brave face on a tough set of circumstances? Seeing two faces could reflect a concern about duplicity—are you or is someone else being two-faced?

POSITIVE INTERPRETATION

Dreaming that you have a beautiful face suggests you feel good about how you are seen by others; this is especially true if your expression is one of happiness. Seeing familiar faces in a dream may indicate that you feel the need for security, or perhaps that a gathering has been planned.

NEGATIVE INTERPRETATION

Dreaming one has an aged or marked face reveals that you have concerns about the way you are seen; perhaps you have a negative characteristic that you worry has become visible to others (Oscar Wilde's story *The Picture of Dorian Gray* taps deeply into this vein of fear and guilt).

A FACELESS PERSON

Dreaming of a faceless figure could represent parts of yourself that are shifting and indefinable—such as changing opinions, a situation that you are unsure of, or any unknown factor in a situation.

LIPS

The lips are an instrument of communication and therefore are often associated with a need to say (or not say) something. Lips can also be a half-disguised symbol of the female genitalia. Wearing lipstick in a dream focuses attention on the lips. Like all makeup, this may be a sign of artifice (or dishonest speech), or it could indicate desire or seduction.

MOUTHS

The mouth can have the same symbolic range as the lips (see below, left). In addition, the mouth can hint at hunger or, its excessive cousin, greed. A genuine smile denotes contentment, but a fake or forced smile could suggest that you may be acting in ways to please others. A very large mouth may suggest being "mouthy" or loud.

NOSES

A diverse symbol, the nose often represents our instinctive sense about a situation: We "sniff out" an opportunity or "follow our noses." They can also represent curiosity or nosiness. Your nose may be out of joint if you feel someone has displaced or slighted you in some way. Alternatively, a nose could suggest something is in plain view (as in the saying "as plain as the nose on your face")—and a nose is also one of many phallic symbols.

CHEEKS

Pink cheeks are a sign of good health and youth, and also of blushing. In a dream, they may also allude to someone being cheeky or "having the cheek" to do something.

HIDING THE FACE

Wearing a mask or a veil that covers the face can intimate we are hiding our true self, or feel the need to conceal our emotions. Taking the mask or veil off demonstrates a readiness to reveal the truth about ourselves.

SEEING A FACE IN THE MIRROR

If you dream that you are looking at your face in the mirror, this can indicate self-awareness or a desire to explore the self. Consider whether the face that you see is yours or not, as this may indicate how well your image represents your feelings about your true self. The mirror itself may have symbolic meaning: What does it represent to you? *(See Mirrors, page 96.)*

▲ The smile of the Mona Lisa has tantalized art historians for centuries. And, likewise, faces in our dreams can convey many complex messages.

EYES

▲ A dream eye most often symbolizes what is seen, or not seen.

In dreams, eyes can be about one's own psyche: The "I" that is the self. Eyes are full of symbolism in religion and mythology—and these same meanings occur over and again in dreams. The eye represents, above all, insight—as in the all-seeing eye of God, often represented as an eye surrounded by rays of light in a triangle; or the third eye, which is the doorway to spiritual understanding in many Eastern religions. Much of your interpretation will depend on the context and mood of the dream.

POSITIVE INTERPRETATION

Having clear eyes or good eyesight in a dream suggests that you are able to see the bigger picture, are displaying clear vision, or perhaps have the foresight to prepare for all eventualities. It could imply that you are going into a situation with your eyes open.

NEGATIVE INTERPRETATION

Being watched can have sinister overtones, especially if you have done something you are ashamed of, or are worried will be discovered. Who is doing the watching and what does he or she symbolize? The idea of an evil eye is prevalent in several cultures and could indicate a belief that there are malevolent forces against you. Having your eyes closed, or being unable to see, suggests that you are avoiding confronting something in your waking life ("turning a blind eye"), or that your perception is clouded.

EYE CONTACT

The first thing to consider here is who is the other person in the dream? Making eye contact is a way of engaging with others, so maintaining it or avoiding someone's gaze can represent how you feel about a particular relationship.

WINKING

When we close one eye we are shutting down half of a pair. So winking or blinking can suggest a problem with one half of a couple or a close partnership. Who or what is the other eye—the other "I"—that is not seeing things as the open eye does?

CRYING

Sometimes a dream is no more than a sleeping memory—and so crying in a dream can be a straightforward expression of grief or sadness. But if the act of crying and the emotion felt in the dream do not fit, then something else is being expressed: Always look to the dream emotion for clues.

EARS

▲ Disembodied ears signify that you do not want to hear what others are saying.

Our sense of hearing allows us to feel the presence of things we cannot see—it is a cipher for intuition. It is also the channel through which we can listen to the needs and experiences of others; dreams about ears often signify our ability to hear advice, praise, or criticism. Secrets are whispered into ears and a dream in which ears are significant may be a reference to rumors or hints that you have barely picked up on waking life. Your willingness to listen can be the key to interpreting these dreams.

POSITIVE INTERPRETATION

Dreaming of ears, especially large or multiple ears, can imply that you are open to new possibilities and are able to understand other people's experiences. Or perhaps your unconscious is advising you to listen to the wise words of others. Cleaning the ears can represent a new readiness to listen.

NEGATIVE INTERPRETATION

There is a superstition that the ears go red when someone is gossiping about us, so red or burning ears in a dream can illustrate a fear that others are talking negatively about you or that you feel guilty about something. Blocked ears or deafness can signal a refusal to hear something important, or that you are isolating yourself from others. Bleeding ears probably mean that you have been deeply wounded by another's words.

EARLOBES

In some cultures the wealthy wear heavy ear jewelry, which results in stretched earlobes. Unusually large earlobes in a dream can therefore signify something to do with wealth. The Buddha, who was born a prince, is often depicted with elongated earlobes, so your dream may also be an indication of spiritual wealth or the compassion that comes from hearing the suffering of others. (*See Jewelry, page 87.*)

WEARING EARPLUGS

Wearing earplugs in a dream suggests that you are trying to insulate yourself from an unwelcome truth, or isolate yourself from others in an unhelpful way.

EARACHE OR INJURY

A dream in which you cut off your ear or suffer from ear pain can be a sign that you are finding others intolerable. If someone else in the dream has an ear removed, this could suggest that you are giving unwanted advice or guidance in your waking life.

TEETH

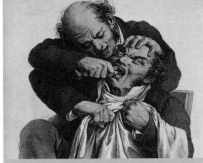

▲ Having a tooth forcibly removed represents a loss of personal control.

Almost everyone has the dream of losing their teeth at some point. This classic dream is usually about some loss of identity or confidence, perhaps a fear of getting older and becoming less attractive, or the loss of your sexual power (which is what Freud put it down to). Sometimes the teeth crumble but stay in your mouth, or you swallow one or more of them. This action can represent a loss that you have been unable to articulate. Loss of teeth dreams often occur at times when a big change involves loss in your life, such as a breakup or moving home.

POSITIVE INTERPRETATION

Teeth are a tool and also a weapon; their appearance can allude to something that you want to "get your teeth into," or a display of personal power. A positive dream about strong teeth or biting through something can reveal that you have confidence in your abilities. A row of healthy teeth may symbolize conformity and goodwill in a group of friends or in the family.

NEGATIVE INTERPRETATION

Dreams of painful teeth may be a straightforward reflection of a dental problem. Struggling to bite into something or having problems with your teeth may show that you are having difficulty making progress with a task in your waking life. The loss of one tooth in a row can symbolize the loss of an important member of a group or family.

FALSE TEETH

If you dream that you are wearing a set of false teeth, consider whether you are presenting an untrue image to the outside world, or being fake in some way.

WISDOM AND BABY TEETH

Wisdom teeth come through in later life and can symbolize maturity and knowledge. Depending on the context of the dream, they can be a positive or negative symbol. Having a baby tooth fall out in a dream may mean you have taken a step toward independence; finding one may represent some aspect of yourself that you have lost in adulthood.

HAVING TEETH REMOVED

Since teeth are a symbol of personal power, having them removed by a dentist or someone else could signify that you have lost control. Who is doing the extraction and what does that figure bring to mind? If you pluck out a tooth yourself, then ask yourself if you are sacrificing something that is important to you.

HAIR

▲ Combing the hair indicates changes in how you present yourself to others.

Flowing locks are a symbol of youth, beauty, and sensuality—particularly for women. Many religions have restrictions or regulations relating to hair: Muslim women cover their hair, as do Christian nuns; monks in various traditions may shave their heads as a sign of humility and abstinence, while Sikhs refrain from cutting their hair. In the Bible, Samson loses his great strength when the temptress Delilah cuts his hair while he is sleeping.

POSITIVE INTERPRETATION

Having long hair can represent freedom; the phrase "let your hair down" means loosening up and having fun. Brushing your hair in a dream could imply that you are working through knotty problems and finding a positive solution. Experimenting with a new hairstyle may show a willingness to try new approaches, or that you are undergoing a change of direction or attitude. Stroking or playing with someone else's hair suggests a wish for intimacy and connection.

NEGATIVE INTERPRETATION

Tangled or knotted hair signals difficulty, and if you find it impossible to manage your hair in a dream then this could highlight a need to find an alternative approach to your current problem. Losing your hair can reflect various anxieties, not necessarily about aging. Wearing a wig can denote falsity, and tightly confined hair suggests denial or restriction.

HAIR BEING CUT

Cutting your own hair can mean you have resolved to remove old attitudes, or perhaps that you are repressing your physical needs. Having your hair cut by someone else, especially if it is against your will, may mean that you are having your emotions ignored or repressed. If you are cutting someone else's hair, consider your attitude to this person in real life.

VISITING THE HAIRDRESSERS

If you dream of going to a hair salon, this may imply that you want to impress others, especially if you are having an elaborate hairstyle. Having your hair colored may show that you want to put on a show, or be more colorful in your ideas.

MUSTACHES AND BEARDS

In a man, facial hair can mean virility or, sometimes, the feminine aspect of a man's personality (as the mouth can represent female genitalia); in a woman, it can suggest her masculine side. Since facial hair obscures the mouth and expression, this can mean you are hiding something.

BLOOD

▲ Bloody hands, such as those of Lady Macbeth, are a powerful dream symbol.

Blood represents the life force, family allegiance, and loyalty to one's own group or people. It is always significant when it appears in dreams. It can also stand for energy and vitality—not just physical, but mental and spiritual as well. Blood is also a means of securing a promise—think of blood brothers or the idea of signing one's name in blood. Dreams of blood can often be positive, especially when the blood is contained within the body.

POSITIVE INTERPRETATION

Blood pumping through your veins suggests that you have the vitality to channel your energies and pursue your passions—it's your unconscious telling you to go for it. Likewise, visiting a blood bank is a suggestion that your energy can easily be replenished. In women, dreams about blood can sometimes be a literal indication that menstruation is starting.

NEGATIVE INTERPRETATION

A hemorrhage can indicate a great sense of loss or depletion, or perhaps an outpouring of emotion. Consider what part of the body the blood is flowing from, since this can give further clues as to the meaning of the dream. If the blood is an unexpected color—blue or green—that suggests some dissonance or imbalance.

BLOOD TRANSFUSIONS

Having a blood transfusion can indicate that you are drawing on fresh energy or being inspired, perhaps by another person. Donating blood yourself can suggest a willingness to share your expertise or interests with another person.

DRINKING BLOOD

This can indicate imbibing strength from another—or perhaps that you have defeated a rival.

BLOOD STAINS

This can suggest guilt, particularly if the blood is on the hands and cannot be removed (consider Shakespeare's Lady Macbeth). If there is blood on an item of clothing, think what that object means to you or reminds you of: That may hint at the meaning of your dream.

SKELETON AND BONES

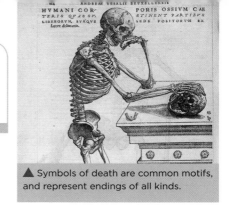

▲ Symbols of death are common motifs, and represent endings of all kinds.

The skeleton is a resilient framework; it gives the body support and structure. A dream in which the bones or skeleton are significant is often about our ability to stand up for ourselves, or to demonstrate will and determination. Since the skeleton is the last part of our bodies to decay after death, it is a frequent symbol of mortality in art and culture. In this way it can represent your feelings about death, or (more likely) the death of some part of yourself.

POSITIVE INTERPRETATION

A dream about the skeleton or bones can be about the structures that support your life: family, routines, and work. We also talk about paring things back to the bone or getting to the bare bones of a situation when we want to focus on the essentials—does this resonate when thinking about your dream's meaning? A dream about bones can alternatively represent intuition, since you can feel it in your bones.

NEGATIVE INTERPRETATION

Dreaming of broken bones could be about damage to your support network, that you either need to avoid or repair. If a particular bone in the body is broken, consider the function and symbolism of this part: A broken arm may suggest you are unable to defend yourself, for example. Something that is close to the bone is emotionally threatening.

THE SPINE

If the spine features prominently in a dream, this could suggest a need or desire to have a metaphorical backbone—meaning that you should display courage or strength of will. Is the spine straight and healthy looking, or crumbling or bent?

RIBS

These bones form a protective shell around the heart, traditionally the seat of our emotions. The ribs in dreams can suggest a need or desire to protect yourself from feelings of vulnerability. In the Bible, Eve is said to have been created from Adam's rib—and so ribs sometimes stand for the relationships between men and women.

BURYING A BONE

Bones outside the body may suggest secrets or old issues. Burying things often represents things we hide deep in the unconscious mind; the act of burying a bone can be a desire to hide a trauma; digging one up can signify that—for good or ill—you are exhuming an old issue, or returning to some matter long obscured.

Actions

FALLING

▲ Falling in a dream can suggest loss of control, or going in the wrong direction.

It's very common to dream that you are falling—particularly in the first few minutes of sleep. Often, a falling dream may be triggered by the natural lowering of the blood pressure and heart rate that occurs when we fall asleep, but falling is also an anxiety dream that suggests you fear failure or feel out of control in a particular area of your life. We need to experience falling many times as a child learning to walk, and it's a danger whenever we explore the steep slopes of our capabilities, the cliff edges of our hopes and ambitions.

POSITIVE INTERPRETATION

A falling dream could be a sign that you should let go of the need to control a situation (or person), and allow things to fall into place naturally. If, in your dream, you find a way to float or land on your feet, this is a sure sign that you can manage the tricky situations you are facing, if you allow it.

NEGATIVE INTERPRETATION

Something that usually provides you with security—your job, your relationship, your finances—is under threat. A falling dream can also suggest that you have fallen short of your own or others' high standards, or that you are worried you have done something that may cause a fall from grace or a loss of reputation.

SOMEONE ELSE FALLING

The cast of characters in your dreams—real or imaginary—often represents aspects of you. If you dream of another person falling, think what this person represents to you and how you felt in the dream about their fall. It could signal fear or desire about relinquishing someone or some facet of yourself.

BEING PUSHED

Who is doing the pushing? Is it someone you feel is pressuring you in real life? If you cannot see the person, it may indicate that you are pushing yourself too hard.

CLINGING ON

Holding on to an edge can indicate the efforts you are making to rectify a situation that is going wrong, even though it is out of your control.

◀ One of the most pleasurable aspects of dreamlife is that we can experience superhuman abilities.

ACTIONS

CLIMBING

▲ Ladders symbolize ascending to a higher stage in some area of life.

Climbing dreams are usually about aspirations and goals, and our progress toward them. The level of ease or difficulty you experience when you are climbing in a dream reflects the level of confidence you have about your ability to meet your goals. There may be obstacles to face along the way, and these could reflect challenges you face in waking life. Reaching the top suggests confidence in your ability to surmount obstacles. Climbing in dreams may be accompanied by a fear of falling (that is, failure), especially when you are up very high; what lies below you may be significant.

POSITIVE INTERPRETATION

Climbing can be seen as a sign of progress; even when the going is difficult, there is a sense of moving toward your goal, especially if the end is in sight. It can be a reminder to take things one step at a time. Alternatively, it can be a reference to advancing your status or climbing higher up the social hierarchy.

NEGATIVE INTERPRETATION

Why are you climbing? Climbing can indicate a wish to escape from something or someone. A lack of progress or never reaching the top indicates a worry that your goal is unattainable or that you do not have the stamina to achieve it.

CLIMBING A LADDER

A ladder can signify spiritual growth; in the Bible Jacob's ladder runs from Earth to heaven. It can also be the ladder of success, progress toward promotion or another career goal.

CLIMBING A HILL

In dreams, a hill can suggest something is more difficult than you expected and you are facing an uphill struggle. A hill can also represent the first half of your life (with downhill being the later stages). (*See Mountains and Hills, page 99.*)

CLIMBING A SCAFFOLD

A scaffold is a temporary structure and can indicate a need for temporary support. Scaffolds have also been places of execution, so there may be a sense that an old part of one's life (or character) needs to die in order for progress to be made.

BEING TRAPPED

▲ This engraving shows an ancient and nightmarish Chinese punishment.

Being trapped and unable to escape is a basic human fear—so it is not surprising that entrapment scenarios often crop up in dreams. Generally, these dreams are a metaphor for feeling imprisoned in some aspect of our waking life, such as work, relationships, or family responsibilities. The dream may be drawing our attention to this if our conscious mind has not acknowledged it, or else suggesting ways to escape the situation.

POSITIVE INTERPRETATION

If you are able to escape your confinement, then this signals confidence that you can overcome the issue in your waking life, or are within touching distance of a new sense of freedom. Being trapped in a dream can also indicate that something needs releasing, such as an emotion, a long-suppressed memory, or perhaps an outdated attitude.

NEGATIVE INTERPRETATION

Dreams about feeling trapped are usually unpleasant and intimate you feel powerless or controlled by other people or life circumstances. As well as indicating frustration, they may suggest that you are wishing to avoid your responsibilities or escape a difficult situation or consequences that have come about as a result of your own actions. Look for clues as to what measures you should take. (*See Buried Alive, page 30.*)

BEING IN A CAGE

Animals are put in cages and this dream can suggest that some primal part of yourself is being confined. The phrase "a bird in a gilded cage" suggests someone trapped in a situation that is outwardly luxurious, but restrictive.

WALLS CLOSING IN

Some analysts believe that this common dream is a stylized memory of being in the birth canal, but more usually it implies that you are feeling squeezed in your life or under pressure from responsibilities. We can build a wall around ourselves as a defense, and this alternative interpretation may be worth considering.

BEING KIDNAPPED

Being kidnapped in a dream implies that you feel constrained by others—who is the kidnapper? What do they represent to you? If someone else is being kidnapped then he or she may represent a characteristic of yourself that is being suppressed or denied. If you are doing the kidnapping then it may be that you are confining yourself unnecessarily.

ACTIONS

FLYING

▲ Taking to the sky is a magical power and the ultimate expression of freedom.

Most people have dreamed that they can fly, and this is often a highly enjoyable and uplifting dream to have. It can mean rising above difficulties and reaching new heights of success or creativity, or it may be the manifestation of a desire for freedom from daily routines. There can be many other interpretations, depending on the context of the dream and how you feel when you are flying. Flying is one of the most popular activities that lucid dreamers choose to participate in *(see Lucid Dreaming, page 15).*

POSITIVE INTERPRETATION

Being able to fly can suggest you have transcended the emotions that tie you down—such as anxiety or doubt—or overcome obstacles. Flying alone represents freedom and independence, which may indicate a new start in your waking life. Flying with another person may indicate sexual desire, or perhaps the wish to be more sexually confident.

NEGATIVE INTERPRETATION

Flying can indicate a desire to be free from the earthbound realities of daily life, or may be a sign that you are neglecting some of your responsibilities—especially if you are escaping someone or something when you take off. Flying too fast, or not being able to stop, could suggest that you are being overindulgent or have started something you can't control.

FLYING UP OR DOWN

If your direction is upward, you are making progress in spiritual or material matters. A downward flight could indicate a determination to get things done—or, sometimes, that fear is causing you to retreat from your goals.

DIFFICULTY FLYING

This indicates that you are feeling tethered or held back in some way. Consider what is preventing you from flying to help you interpret this dream.

LOOKING DOWN

Looking at the landscape below suggests you have a broad perspective on life and can see where you are heading. If the view represents something specific (such as work or family) it may be that you have found a new perspective on a situation that has been worrying you. *(See Airplanes, page 82.)*

BEING CHASED

▲ In Greek myth, Daphne calls for divine help to escape the pursuit of Apollo.

Escape is a primal defense strategy. When faced with an aggressor, we have to make a swift choice: to fight or take flight. It is not surprising then, that being chased is one of our most common dreams. These dreams are generally anxiety dreams that suggest you are running away from something in your waking life. Who is chasing you—a person or a group of people, an animal or monster? What might they represent? Consider how threatened you feel and what strategies you use in trying to evade the chaser. This can indicate how well you are dealing with the situation in real life.

POSITIVE INTERPRETATION

If you are doing the chasing, then contemplate what you are pursuing in real life, and your feelings when, or if, you catch your prey in the dream. Chasing a person you are attracted to can be an expression of desire, especially if the chase feels exciting ("the thrill of the chase"), but could also be a sign of suppressed aggressive feelings. If your prey is unidentified or unclear in the dream then your efforts in your waking life may be equally unfocused.

NEGATIVE INTERPRETATION

Being chased is usually an unpleasant and threatening experience. An animal chasing you represents primal emotions, such as anger or lust, that perhaps feel out of control or frightening in some way.

FOLLOWING OR BEING FOLLOWED

If you dream you are following a person or group, or perhaps an animal, then this suggests you are being led by whatever the leader represents on a symbolic level. Being followed suggests that you are taking a lead.

AN UNKNOWN CHASER

Sometimes the chaser in a dream may be a shadowy figure, which can suggest an issue from your past has resurfaced and you do not wish to face it.

BEING CHASED BY A PERSON

This can suggest a fear of commitment or intimacy, or may hint that you are affected by feelings about a past relationship. The chaser can symbolize an aspect of yourself that you are trying to escape, so consider what qualities you associate with this person.

ACTIONS

WASHING

▲ This painting shows a monk washing the feet of Christ, an act of humility.

The act of washing is about more than hygiene—it is a ritual activity in many cultures (usually before worship), signifying new beginnings and a change in the mindset. Since water denotes the emotions and the unconscious, it matters what the water is like in the dream: Is it clean or murky? And is there anything in the water? Where you are washing may also be significant. If it is in a place that you recognize, what associations do you have with that place?

POSITIVE INTERPRETATION

Cleaning is usually a positive act of purification, and may suggest some radical change of heart or direction, or perhaps a desire to be forgiven. Washing in a bathroom or other private space could be related to self-nurture, while washing other people suggests caring for them or dealing with difficulties in your relationships.

NEGATIVE INTERPRETATION

Washing or bathing in dirty water suggests you feel unable to resolve some muddy issue. Think about the pun potential of what you are cleaning in the dream and if wordplay could shed more light on the deeper meaning of the dream.

WASHING THE FEET

Washing someone else's feet is an act of devotion and humility in many religions. Whose feet are you washing, or is it your feet that are being washed?

WASHING THE HANDS

This act is associated with freeing oneself of guilt, or it may be a visual reference to the idea of washing your hands of a situation—in the sense of denying responsibility of it.

DOING THE LAUNDRY

Laundry could be a metaphor for personal or family affairs; dirty laundry suggests that something needs attending to. The saying "washing one's dirty linen in public" could be significant—has private information about you been exposed? The type of dirt or stains on the laundry may help to pinpoint the meaning of the dream. A washing machine in a dream may indicate some kind of emotional turbulence, or a cycle of events.

HAVING SEX

▲ A kiss may reveal a need to embody some aspect of the other person.

Freud believed that the unconscious mind—and the dreamscape of each individual—was largely concerned with unresolved issues around sex. Most psychologists now question this, but would agree with Freud that sex dreams are sometimes what he called "wish fulfillment." Much of the time, though, sex in dreams is symbolic of something else entirely and not a literal expression of a sexual desire. Understanding this fact makes it easier to accept the bizarre or unsettling dream scenarios that sometimes occur.

POSITIVE INTERPRETATION

A sex dream may signify a union between two different sides of your personality. Positive dreams about sex can show an acceptance of your sexual needs, or could be a way of exploring desires that you might feel embarrassed about in waking life. A sex dream can also reveal insights into feelings of vulnerability and power. Sexual experimentation in a dream reveals a wish to explore boundaries in real life.

NEGATIVE INTERPRETATION

Dreaming about unpleasant sex can reveal aspects of your desires that are unacceptable to you in some way. Dreaming can be a safe way of exploring these fantasies. If you have experienced harmful sexual contact in the past, then unpleasant sex dreams may be a sign that you need help with healing.

UNFAMILIAR PLACES OR PRACTICES

An unusual setting could be your unconscious's way of telling you to break out of your waking routine, or may be a sign that you are uncomfortable about risks you are taking, depending on your attitude in the dream.

AN INAPPROPRIATE PARTNER

What characteristics does this person embody? This dream suggests that you are cultivating these characteristics within yourself, or want to. Sex with a celebrity implies a desire for the things that you associate with that person (who may well be someone you dislike in life). Incest dreams are surprisingly common: Sex with a parent may signal your transition to adulthood; sex with other relatives may reflect a need for greater intimacy.

KISSING

Kissing denotes love, affection, and romance. It can represent partnership, or reconciliation—or could perhaps be a goodbye kiss. The person you are kissing could represent some aspect of yourself that you need to integrate within.

ACTIONS

BEING NAKED

▲ Nudity can be a beautiful expression of freedom, as in Modigliani's painting.

Being naked in a dream is not often connected with sexuality; it usually concerns issues of vulnerability or empowerment. It can be a very literal metaphor for feeling or being exposed, since we use clothes to cover up. Being nude in a public place is a classic dream about inhibition. If you are happy and relaxed, then this suggests you feel free to express yourself and be accepted by others. If you are ashamed and others are mocking you—which is more common—then this reflects waking worries about how you are perceived. If only part of you is exposed, consider what this part may symbolize *(see The Human Body, pages 17–45)*.

POSITIVE INTERPRETATIONS

Feeling happy in a naked dream implies that you are comfortable in your own skin and are content with who you are, or it could be a way of encouraging yourself to be more open with others. Nakedness is a sign of innocence—think of small children and their relaxed approach to nudity, or the many creation stories in which the world's first humans were naked. Dreams of nudity may reflect a wish to return to the carefree days of childhood.

NEGATIVE INTERPRETATIONS

Feeling ashamed or vulnerable while naked in a public place suggests you feel uncomfortable about revealing some part of yourself; what is it that you wish to hide from others?

SEEING OTHERS NAKED

If you feel disapproval toward a naked person in your dream, or he or she is trying to hide from you, perhaps this person has deceived you in real life or you are worried that you have betrayed a confidence or exposed something about him or her? Feeling positive toward a naked person suggests that you have got to know some hitherto hidden truth about him or her (or what he or she represents).

BEING INVISIBLE

Invisibility indicates that you feel disregarded or unable to make your presence felt in your waking life. Or perhaps you are keeping your opinions or feelings hidden from others and it is time to reveal them? Invisibility dreams are often accompanied by a sense of power: When you are invisible you are very nearly invincible.

COMMUNICATING

▲ A bad line suggests you are struggling to hear an important message.

The unconscious mind likes to argue with itself, and so dreams can sometimes take the form of conversations or even altercations. A blazing row in a dream often points to an inner conflict that you are experiencing in your waking life. The two people arguing in the dream may represent different sides of yourself, or opposing facets of a difficult decision that you are facing.

POSITIVE INTERPRETATION

If you receive a message in a dream, consider the wording carefully to see whether a deeper meaning is hidden within a pun or wordplay. If you receive a letter in a dream, are you pleased to get it and do you open it? If you ignore it, then perhaps there is something you are neglecting in your waking life.

NEGATIVE INTERPRETATION

Whispering or opening your mouth but being unable to speak, can suggest that you feel silenced in real life or unable to vocalize your feelings. This is also the case if someone is preventing you from speaking, or is talking over you. Being shouted at may be a warning that you are ignoring the needs of others and need to pay better attention.

TELEPHONES

Telephones focus the mind on exactly what one has to say and listening to the other person. A telephone can represent a message that needs to be heard. Who is the person on the other end of the line? Is it someone who is hard to get through to in real life? Unanswered or disconnected calls, or wrong numbers, can represent difficulties in communicating, or an inability to contact someone, perhaps because he or she has died or is no longer in your life.

NOTICES

If a message appears on a noticeboard, this could be your unconscious ensuring that you pay attention. Look at the wording, and think about details such as the handwriting or the kind of paper used.

PUBLIC SPEAKING

Dreams about public speaking are common, and are often anxiety dreams. If you are standing before a large audience or speaking through a microphone, this can be a dream about social status, and the hope that you can command the respect of others.

BEING TESTED

▲ Exam dreams often occur when you feel scrutinized or emotionally tested.

Many people dream of tests or examinations, perhaps because school tests are one of our earliest experiences of performance anxiety, so it is a useful symbol of stress for the unconscious to draw on. This is a dream that usually contains clues to an anxiety in waking life, but it can also suggest you are ready to move up a level—perhaps you are seeking a promotion at work or want to take on new responsibilities, and are questioning whether you are capable. The circumstances of the dream test can give you clues to the dream's underlying meaning.

POSITIVE INTERPRETATION

Having success in a test, or finding it easy to complete the test, suggests that you have the necessary resources to deal with a current challenge. You are measuring yourself against others and feel satisfied that you are meeting or exceeding expectations.

NEGATIVE INTERPRETATION

Dreaming of an exam can indicate that you feel under pressure or are being tested or criticized in your waking life. You may dream that you go blank, are completely unprepared, or are looking at blank sheet of paper—symbolizing your belief that you are not equipped for the challenges you currently face.

CHEATING IN AN EXAM

This points to your involvement in a deception in your waking life. Your unconscious may be warning you to desist from unethical behavior. If someone else is cheating, this implies you feel someone has an unfair advantage over you.

ROAD TESTS

Driving a car is a metaphor for steering your way through life; undergoing a road test therefore suggests there is doubt (either from yourself or those close to you) about your ability to navigate your life's path, or that you are unsure about some new direction. (*See Cars, pages 78–79.*)

MEDICAL TESTS

If you dream you are subject to medical tests then this may be a picture of some self-assessment that you are undergoing, or feel that you should undergo. The part of the body is significant: Are you "looking to your heart," "trying your arm," or being urged to "have your head examined"?

HAVING SURGERY

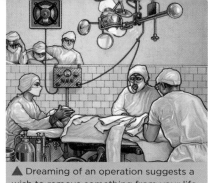

▲ Dreaming of an operation suggests a wish to remove something from your life.

Dreams of surgery are often about the need to repair something in your life, or perhaps to cut someone or something out of it altogether. The key to interpreting the dream may be the part of the body that is being operated on—what does this signify? The identity of the surgeon may also be significant. Think too about the wide-ranging meaning of the word "operation": Might the dream refer to some project you are involved in or some group endeavor from your past?

POSITIVE INTERPRETATION

Surgery dreams may be a call for incisive change—an intervention that may be difficult but is ultimately healing. You may be encouraged to focus on an area of your life that is being neglected or needs extra care.

NEGATIVE INTERPRETATION

Dreaming of undergoing surgery can be frightening, especially if you do not consent to what is happening. It can indicate feelings of powerlessness, particularly if you dream that you are under anesthetic. Perhaps, for example, an authority figure in your waking life is causing you to behave in ways that you feel uncomfortable with.

HEART SURGERY

A dream of heart surgery could be a message from your unconscious that it is time to open up your heart and reveal more of yourself to other people or create space for greater emotional growth.

COSMETIC SURGERY

This could represent a longing to change your self-image or the way you are perceived in the outside world. Is the part of your body undergoing surgery one that you would want to change in waking life? If not, think what else this cosmetic operation might imply.

BRAIN SURGERY

A dream involving brain surgery suggests that you are seeking insights into your unconscious mind. Brain surgery is something proverbially difficult (like rocket science); is your self-exploration feeling too hard to cope with at this juncture?

People and Places

THE HERO

▲ The hero occurs in many forms—here as St. George slaying the dragon.

We all know stories in which a hero faces a mortal enemy, fights for his life, emerges triumphant, and then returns home to tell his tale. In all its forms, the hero narrative is a dramatization of the journey of overcoming difficulty in order to grow and progress— something we all do again and again in life. In a dream, the hero narrative reminds us that whatever we are going through is one stage in a process. It can also be a call to extend yourself to the utmost of your ability and fulfill your potential, or perhaps it is an expression of the confidence you currently feel.

POSITIVE INTERPRETATION

If you dream that you are defeating an enemy, this signals that you have taken a step forward psychologically, or are about to. The reassuring message from your unconscious is that you are more powerful than you think. The powers you use and the foe you defeat in the dream may represent aspects of your own psyche.

NEGATIVE INTERPRETATION

If, in your dream, you take on an enemy and lose, this could indicate that you are unready for some psychological ordeal. If someone else is the hero in your dream, then this implies you are somehow shirking your waking responsibilities (perhaps to yourself) and allowing someone else to take center stage. A hero dream can also signify one's need to be a rescuer in waking life.

◀ Our dreams are peopled by loved ones, by strangers, or by mythical or celebrity figures—all helping to convey a message from the unconscious mind.

SUPERHUMAN STRENGTH

When people dream of having superhuman strength—being able to smash through walls or destroy obstacles—this is an indication that they have made touch with reserves of power within themselves. This inner strength, not physical but moral or emotional, is the key to resolving some pressing situation in waking life.

EXTREME SPEED

This superhuman attribute has a dual aspect: It can be exhilarating or terrifying. Consider whether your psyche is showing you that you can outstrip your opponents (and if so, how); or whether the message is that you are moving too fast, perhaps with a relationship or some irreversible course of action.

MYTHICAL CHARACTERS

Mythical characters usually epitomize some human characteristic, such as loyalty or determination. When they appear in dreams, your unconscious is usually urging you to take on this characteristic and apply it to your current situation.

PEOPLE AND PLACES

FATHER FIGURE

▲ Your feelings about authority may be played out with a dream father figure.

In Freudian psychology, confrontation with the father is part of the process through which the psyche finds itself: To become the best version of oneself, one must move beyond the naivety and the risk-free environment that one knew under the care of one's parents. Dreams of father figures can also be a way of working through issues that you have with your own father or with another authority figure, and of confronting aspects of oneself that have been inherited from this person.

POSITIVE INTERPRETATION

A father figure in a dream can represent all the traditional positive aspects of that parental relationship: protection, physical strength, good counsel, decisiveness, a helping hand, and practical skills. The dream could be allowing you to investigate how you are using these skills in your waking life. If your actual father was unkind or absent, a genial father in a dream may be a mechanism to heal feelings of loss or pain.

NEGATIVE INTERPRETATION

If a dreamer's waking relationship with their own father is bad, or if the dreamer has negative feelings about issues of abandonment, disapproval, or resentment, then the father figure in a dream can represent these troubled emotions or an anxiety about being dominated or unloved. An angry or sad father could suggest recognition that you have made a poor decision.

FATHERLY REPROACH

Fathers can stand for conscience; before a child develops a sense of right and wrong, it takes its cues from the praise or prohibitions that a parent figure lays down. This makes them a perfect symbol of one's own moral awareness once it has developed and become internalized. As such, the death of a father figure in a dream can refer to a loss of one's moral awareness or to a need to step up to a more authoritative role.

A GRANDFATHER FIGURE

Any grandfather-like figure in a dream is likely to represent the archetype of the Wise Old Man (represented by Santa Claus, Gandalf in Tolkien's *The Lord of the Rings*, and other such characters). You should listen carefully to what this dream character says.

STRUGGLING WITH A FATHER

It is common to dream of fighting one's father. This is a dream about moving past the childish wish to be directed and cared for, and striking out on one's own.

MOTHER FIGURE

▲ Raphael's image encapsulates the bond between the Madonna and child.

There is perhaps no dream figure more universal or more profound than the mother. In our psyche, the mother is the source of life, the fount of love, and the human image of nurture and protection. Having said that, the mother archetype can take many forms; she is almost infinitely variable and open to interpretation—and not all maternal figures are entirely positive.

POSITIVE INTERPRETATION

Mothers can stand for all that is good about the traditional maternal role: the all-enveloping care, the comfort, the familiarity. Someone who has a painful relationship with their own mother may dream of a more pleasing parental figure in order to heal a sense of pain. More generally, the mother figure represents emotional satisfaction and guidance through intuition. The advice offered by a dream mother is worth paying attention to.

NEGATIVE INTERPRETATION

The folk figure of the wicked stepmother symbolizes what happens when motherhood goes wrong, when the flow of maternal love becomes blocked. If you dream of a threatening mother figure—a real person or a fictional character—then it may be that you are feeling starved of the affection a mother represents, that you are contending with jealousy from some quarter, or that you feel controlled or suffocated emotionally.

AN IDEALIZED MOTHER

Ideal mother figures crop up frequently in dreams and in popular culture. Mrs. March from *Little Women* is an ideal figure, as is the Virgin Mary of Christianity, elevated to the divine plane. Dreams of such figures may represent a longing for unconditional love and total protection.

AN EARTH MOTHER

The concept of the earth mother connects the maternal image with the abundance and the fecundity of the earth. Dreams of an earth mother (she may be someone who has a connection to the land, such as a traveler or traditional gypsy, a hippie, or a farmer) can be about creativity, growth, or some kind of emotional fulfillment.

THE DEATH OF A MOTHER

This dream may reflect waking fears or a sense of loss if you have been bereaved in real life. It can also signify that you feel disconnected from your intuitive side, or perhaps that you have moved on from a difficult relationship with your actual mother. (*See Pregnancy, page 23.*)

ROYALTY

▲ The king is the ultimate father figure and epitome of masculine authority.

We all reign supreme in our own consciousness. It is almost impossible not to see oneself as the center of the universe, as the most important character in one's own story. Dreams of royalty are often about the ego, the centrality of the self. Commonly, people dream that they are hiding the fact that they are a king or queen. This is an acknowledgment of the awareness that others do not see us as being quite as important as we do ourselves.

POSITIVE INTERPRETATION

The king or queen in your dream—even if it is you—may not represent you in your entirety. It may be some aspect of yourself that is presently in the ascendancy; perhaps it reflects a recent burst of confidence or a change of character wrought by success. This last interpretation is especially likely if you see yourself ascending to the throne through some struggle. Kings and queens also represent masculine and feminine strength, and the power to grant desires and bring about change in your life.

NEGATIVE INTERPRETATION

Dreams of royalty or becoming royal can also be a reproach from the unconscious mind, a hint that perhaps you are overreaching yourself or being arrogant. Check how you feel about your elevated status within the dream context: Is there a sense of uneasiness or a suggestion that you do not deserve to be wearing that crown? If someone else is the royal figure, do you experience feelings of being unworthy, or at the mercy of a capricious authority figure?

PRINCES AND PRINCESSES

A princess can stand for all that is best in the anima, the female aspect of the psyche, while a prince can symbolize the same for the animus, the male aspect.

THRONES

A throne often represents some aspect of your life where you feel in total control. Try to describe the throne to yourself. Say it is made of silver, which puts you in mind of a brooch given to you by your mother: Perhaps you feel unconsciously that the dynamic of the mother-child relationship has shifted your way and you now have more control.

THE CROWN AND SCEPTER

A crown is a common symbol of authority. Consider who is wearing the crown in your dream and what might that person represent? A scepter can be a phallic symbol and, because of its royal nature, might represent an overpowering sexual urge.

SERVANTS

▲ Being served could reflect a need to be nourished and let others do the work.

Dreaming that you are a maid or servant suggests that you are putting the needs of others before your own in your waking life, or are in a circumstance that forces you to do so. This may reflect a general feeling that your obligations are preventing you from fulfilling yourself, or it can be a dream of inferiority or even humiliation. If you are being served by others, consider how this made you feel in the dream—are you disregarding the feelings of those you feel are beneath you, or acknowledging the support that you receive?

POSITIVE INTERPRETATION

If, in your dream, you gain satisfaction from serving others this can suggest that you are using your energies well in your waking life. Religions often speak of serving God and this concept of giving service may be reflected in your dream.

NEGATIVE INTERPRETATION

Being a servant in a dream may be a symbol of financial dependence or of being trapped in a situation that you cannot escape from, especially if you are a slave. Treating servants badly in a dream suggests that you are putting excessive demands on someone else.

SERVING AT A TABLE

Dreams in which you cater to the needs of others could be an affirmation of a positive role that you fulfill in your waking life, offering sustenance to others.

SERVILITY

Dreams that you are in an unpleasantly servile situation—working in a lowly job for a domineering master or mistress, for example—suggest that some part of you is in thrall to a force that you cannot overcome, or at least in danger of such a thing. That powerful force could be internal, an addiction of some kind, or an obsessive compulsion.

BEING SERVED

If you are enjoying being served by others in your dream, this suggests you have supportive and helpful relationships. The servant may symbolize something that has made your life easier, such as working from home instead of commuting. Or perhaps it is a suggestion that you need to make your needs clear to others.

COURT AND PRISON

Dreams about being in court or about breaking the law are not generally concerned with legality but with morality: They concern the rules that govern the way we live. We all internalize these rules at a very young age, with the result that we can feel guilty even when we do something that may be unconventional, but is not in any way wrong. Our dreams provide us with a way to explore and move past these conflicted feelings, and are a useful vehicle that enables us to admit things that we are too ashamed of to acknowledge in our waking lives.

POSITIVE INTERPRETATION

Dreams to do with judgment generally suggest that you are assessing either your own or someone else's behavior; being found not guilty is a message of vindication. If you are being judged in your dream, this could also relate to a wider sense of being judged in real life—are you going for an interview or being tested in some other way?

NEGATIVE INTERPRETATION

Dream crimes relate to transgressions in our waking life, which may be against other people or against our true nature. If you receive a harsh punishment in the dream, this usually represents the level of guilt you feel. If you steal something in a dream, this suggests that someone is being dishonest in your waking life. It could also mean that your energy is being diverted ("stolen") by something or someone that is not worthwhile. *(See Killing and Violent Death, pages 30–31.)*

THE COURTROOM

Dreaming that you are a prisoner in the dock defending yourself against charges, suggests that you are struggling with an issue concerning fairness or guilt in your waking life. A lawyer is someone who argues for the defense or the prosecution—which side gained the upper hand in your dream?

JUDGES

A judge represents the part of ourselves that criticizes and judges, and can also symbolize any authority figure in our lives. Who is the dream judge? If it is someone you know (either directly or indirectly) then consider if the characteristics that this person embodies are significant.

SCALES

Traditionally, scales are the symbol of justice, with which one must weigh up both sides of an argument before giving judgment. In a dream, scales can represent an important decision that needs careful consideration.

POLICE OFFICERS

A police officer is an instrument of the law and of the moral codes of the society we live in. When an officer appears in a dream their presence may point to an unease that you are transgressing the social norms, or the need to keep yourself in check in order not to offend others. The emphasis in such dreams is on fitting in rather than following one's instincts and personal values.

GUARDS

Within a dream a guard could be cast in the role of a jailer, there to prevent some reckless or irresponsible part of you from getting out. But guards can also protect important treasure, which in a dream could relate to

some hidden part of the psyche. Does the dream give a hint about what is being guarded? Or is this dream revealing a need for greater security in your life?

▲ Being behind bars could reflect a sense that you have confined yourself, perhaps unnecessarily.

JAIL IMPRISONMENT

This is synonymous with confinement and loss of freedom, which may relate to your current circumstances. A jailer may be the part of your psyche that restricts your freedom in some way—perhaps your creativity is being stifled?— or may represent someone who is blocking or restricting your progress.

WITCHES
AND WIZARDS

▲ Is your dream witch full of magic and mischief, or sinister and manipulative?

Witches in dreams can represent the dark side of the earth mother archetype (*see Mother Figure, page 61*). A wizard has admirable powers and abilities, but can also be manipulative and amoral. Supernatural beings generally represent our shadow side, which Jung described as "everything that the subject refuses to acknowledge about himself." A dream encounter with the shadow can be terrifying or disturbing, but acknowledgment of this part of ourselves is an important stage in "individuation," the process whereby people become self-aware and the best possible version of themselves.

POSITIVE INTERPRETATION

Witches and wizards have the power to perform spells and create magic, which can be transformational. In a dream they may be able to see the future, and thus may be a source of important advice. A witch is also a wise woman, a mother figure, symbolizing intuition and healing.

NEGATIVE INTERPRETATION

A witch can represent a woman who is making you unhappy (perhaps deliberately so) or manipulating you—it's not uncommon to dream of your own mother or mother-in-law as a witch if you are feeling put-upon. If you dream that you yourself are a witch, then this could be an acknowledgment of your own attempts to control others by dubious means. The selfish trickster wizard could also represent an aspect of yourself or a malign presence in your life.

DEMONS

Often another outworking of the shadow side, demons in dreams may represent our own character demons—traits such as addictive tendencies, a short temper, or bad moods.

ANGELS AND DEVILS

These figures are likely to represent the good and bad in oneself, and the struggle for supremacy between these two halves. The dream may be a way of illustrating an upcoming decision in which you have to choose between self-interest and a more ethical stance.

GHOSTS

A ghost is generally some faint aspect or memory of another person, who is perhaps deceased but may simply no longer be present in our life. A ghost in a dream may also represent a character trait—positive or negative—that you have almost, but not quite, eradicated.

PLACES OF
WORSHIP

▲ Religious buildings are places of tranquility as well as moral guidance.

If you dream that you are in a church or other place of worship such as a mosque or temple, it may indicate that you are seeking out spiritual comfort. Places of worship also represent a moral code, and your dream could be suggesting that you are in need of ethical guidance. You might dream of a place of worship that you are familiar with, or one that represents a different faith from your own—consider what you associate with the particular building or the religion it represents. People have traditionally sought sanctuary in places of worship, so a longing for security or protection could also be the meaning behind your dream.

POSITIVE INTERPRETATION

Places of worship can symbolize feelings of self-worth. If the dream is positive and involves images of revelation (these can be spectacular, such as choirs of angels, or more suggestive, such as a shaft of light through a window), then this could point to a breakthrough in the dreamer's own sense of self.

NEGATIVE INTERPRETATION

A dream of desecration—damaging or defiling a church or its symbols—could be a dream about rejecting old beliefs, possibly beliefs about oneself, and acknowledging that the process will be difficult or painful. Being outside the church suggests that you are evaluating your beliefs from an objective point of view. A negative dream involving a place of worship could also allude to some guilt or repentance that you harbor.

PRAYING AND CONFESSING

We pray in times of crisis, so this can be an expression of need and a desire for help. It can also imply that you are seeking sanction for some desired course of action, perhaps one that you know to be morally dubious. Confessing in a dream can signify guilt or a desire to make amends.

PRIESTS

Spiritual leaders can be a positive embodiment of the guru archetype. Dreamers often encounter priest-like figures when they are involved in some kind of spiritual exploration. A dream that a religious figure offers absolution implies self-acceptance, while being berated by a priest-like figure is a sign of wrongdoing and guilt.

RELIGIOUS SYMBOLS

A symbol such as a cross in a dream can be a call to investigate one's spiritual life more fully.

BUILDINGS AND CITIES

Town and cities are like our dreams in that they are worlds that we build for ourselves, to suit our needs or to reflect our aspirations. It follows that the built environment provides a rich source of symbolism that the unconscious can draw on when we sleep. The architecture of the mind can be fantastical, mundane, familiar, or exotic—but, like all the sets and scenery of our dreams, it is there to tell us something about ourselves.

POSITIVE INTERPRETATION

Nostalgic dreams about familiar places indicate a sense of contentment about the past. The content of the dream can reveal whether there are still lessons to be learned from this period of your life. Familiar landscapes can also represent your usual ways of dealing with a situation. Feeling comfortable in a city or town indicates that you feel happy about your place in society.

NEGATIVE INTERPRETATION

Sometimes a nostalgic dream intimates that you are unhappy in your current situation and yearn for a simpler time. In dreams, as in waking life, the city can be a place of isolation and looming danger: If you dream of a city that is dark and threatening, it may be that you are feeling overwhelmed by the troubles you are tackling. Finding your way around an unfamiliar city suggests that you need to try a new approach to a current issue.

SKYSCRAPERS

Tall narrow buildings are unmistakable phallic symbols—an assertion of masculine power. In dreams, they can represent sexual desire and energy, as well as a more general urge that is about creativity, ambition, and the desire to make a mark, especially if the dream is of building a skyscraper.

CASTLES

Typically, castles are designed to have concentric rings of defense: the moat, the battlements and walls, and the innermost keep. In this way a castle in a dream can be a metaphor for the personality and the way in which we let people approach us—get past our defenses—one stage at a time.

HOSPITALS

Hospitals are places of healing. If you dream of undergoing or administering treatment, or of performing or having an operation, then the chances are that you are both doctor and patient. In such dreams your psyche is dramatizing some process of psychological healing that you are making happen for yourself, or could make happen if you wanted to. If you are lost in a hospital that might indicate that you have yet to identify what is ailing your spirit and how you might cure it.

HOTELS

By definition a hotel is a temporary place to stay. If you dream of an unspecified hotel or motel, this may suggest that you are at a halfway house on some emotional or psychological journey.

STORES

Dreams of stores often concern some quality that you feel you lack or wish to acquire. Perhaps you long for inner strength, and so in your dream find yourself buying spinach (like the

cartoon character Popeye the Sailor) or strong flour. What store are you in? If you dream of trying to buy strong flour in a hair salon, for example, this can be an indication that in waking life you are seeking for self-improvement in the wrong quarter.

WAREHOUSES AND BARNS

Dreams of warehouses or barns can be a representation of the great storehouse of the mind—the place where all your memories, thoughts, hopes, worries, neuroses, loves, and plans are tucked away. The purpose of these dreams is to revisit some dusty memory, unpack it, face it, and unravel it, thereby neutralizing its

▲ Dreaming of a building that is collapsing may reflect feelings that the structure of your life is falling apart.

power over you. Your barn or warehouse dream may be pointing the way to achieve this.

FACTORIES

Things are assembled in factories, often on an assembly line. This dream setting can indicate repetitive ways of doing things: Habits and routines, or monotony. But it can also be a metaphor for teamwork and efficiency.

SCHOOL

▲ A strict teacher reflects a feeling of being bullied in your waking life.

School is usually the first place that we learn to conform to a set of rules outside of the family. They are a place where we are measured against others and where we learn our place in a social hierarchy, all while navigating the difficult business of transitioning from childhood to adolescence. And they are, of course, places of learning and development, where we discover new knowledge and test ourselves. Most people have vivid memories of their schooldays and so it is not surprising that we return to them in our dreams.

POSITIVE INTERPRETATION

A school dream suggests that you are absorbing new information, learning, and developing, or perhaps that you are desirous of intellectual stimulation. It could also mean that you are thinking of a current situation in your waking life and what you can learn from it.

NEGATIVE INTERPRETATION

If your memories of school are unhappy, then this dream can be a way of working through the residual emotions and insecurities. It may be that a current situation is triggering these memories (if you were bullied at school, then conflict at work may remind you of the feelings of powerlessness that you experienced here). School settings, and examinations in particular, can relate to worries about performance or being tested (see Being Tested, page 56).

LESSONS

Attending a particular lesson in your dream could be an indication of what you should be focusing on in waking life. A gym lesson could be a way of encouraging yourself to exercise, a history lesson might point to some examination of the past, and a math lesson could be suggesting that logic or some kind of lateral thinking is needed.

TEACHERS

A good teacher is one who imparts knowledge and inspires you—another example of the guru archetype. In a dream this character could be pointing toward some important lesson or insight. A teacher is also someone who has control over you when you are relatively powerless, so this can also be a dream about authority and leadership issues.

WORK

Dreaming of homework is a warning that you are taking your work home with you, perhaps to the detriment of your family relationships. It can also serve as a metaphor for excuses—is there something that you haven't done?

WORKPLACE

▲ Desks represent important business, work on yourself, or decision-making.

Dreaming about work is very common. If you dream of your own work setting then your dream probably reflects your actual work. But work dreams can also represent other aspects of our lives. Looking for a job in a dream can signify a wish to improve your status or to find some worthwhile way to spend your time; or it may be a message that there is a job that needs doing, or that you need to work on your spiritual or emotional development. Getting a new job can represent a new phase of life or a feeling that you are worth more than your current circumstances offer. (*See Buildings and Cities, pages 68–69.*)

POSITIVE INTERPRETATION

A positive dream that melds past and present workplaces suggests that you are using your experience to make a success of your current job (or should be). Dreaming that you have a relationship with a colleague could indicate that you should work with them for a common cause, or that he or she has some worthwhile attribute that you would like to cultivate in yourself. On a more literal level, this dream could also be a wish-fulfillment dream if you are attracted to that person.

NEGATIVE INTERPRETATION

Anxiety work dreams are common. Being late for work suggests you feel that you are missing out on a career opportunity, as can being in an elevator that has stopped. Not being able to find the restroom suggests that basic needs are not being met by your job. (*See Being Naked, page 54.*)

CROWDED WORKPLACE

If your dream workplace is full of furniture or bustling with people, this suggests that work issues are becoming overwhelming for you.

DESKS

In dreams, a desk is a clear symbol of focus and implies that you are getting down to business. Important papers may be stored in desk drawers or in filing cabinets, so these items could refer to information about yourself that you are concealing or protecting.

BOSS FIGURES

Dreaming of your boss may indicate authority and leadership, which can be a positive aspect of yourself. However, this could also be a dream of feeling put upon or perhaps bossed about by someone in your life.

HOUSES AND ROOMS

In dreams, the house is a picture of the self—its rooms, the many chambers, stairways, and corridors of our thoughts, desires, and emotions. The things that happen within the dream house, especially if it is a version of your own home, are an indication of the busy processes going on inside your own mind, and each room signifies a different part of your psyche. The modern parts of a dream house can relate to your current circumstances, with older parts relating to childhood.

POSITIVE INTERPRETATION

If you are happily exploring a house, this indicates that you are at peace with your psyche. It is common to dream of homes you lived in as a child. If the dreams feel happy or nostalgic, this is a sign that you have resolved any childhood issues that once caused you pain. Discovering a new room indicates that you are discovering some new dimension of yourself.

NEGATIVE INTERPRETATION

Dreaming that you are in a house that is falling down is an indication of psychological upset. A haunted house may point to unresolved issues with family or some aspect of your past. Blocked windows imply that you are blind to some aspect of yourself, while blocked doors suggest either an inability to communicate ("open up"), or some impediment to your progress.

CORRIDORS

Corridors and hallways often represent transition. Door-lined corridors in houses are a clear representation of a range of choices facing you. Why are these choices not shown as a crossroads or an open box of chocolates? Because all the options available to you are unknowns; you do not know what lies behind the closed doors.

KITCHENS AND HEARTHS

Fireplaces are a traditional source of warmth and also the place where cooking (creativity) happens. Kitchens and hearths therefore stand for the same things in dreams: They are about the aspects of life that sustain you, that warm your soul, or are of vital importance to you.

BEDROOMS

A dream of a bedroom or of being in bed often represents the childlike desire to return to the womb. In Freudian psychology, this return is often connected to the experience of unrequited love—could that be the meaning of your dream? It can also be linked to an awareness of death, which is a return to a state of affairs that existed before we were born. (*See Beds, page 94.*)

LOFTS OR ATTICS

The high parts of a house naturally symbolize the higher functions of the mind: intellect, reason, and intelligence. So a dream of living in an attic might suggest that you are focused on the rational sphere. If you find treasure hidden in an attic, that might suggest that the answer to a problem is attainable—you just need to puzzle it out. Attics can also represent memories, since this is where we store unwanted belongings from our past; a dream of clearing an attic may suggest resolving past issues.

BATHROOMS AND TOILETS

The bathroom is the place where we are most likely to be naked and, in a dream context, these rooms represent the exposure of things that we would rather keep hidden or that are repressed

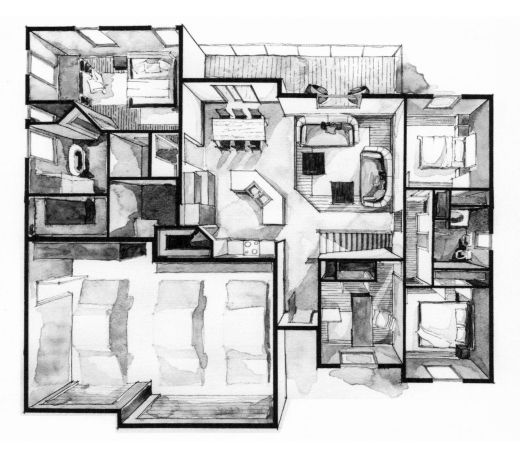

by the mind. This is especially apparent if the fear of exposure is dramatized by the dream narrative—for example, if someone is battering at the door when you are in the bath.

LOCKED DOORS

The unconscious mind monitors our attempts to unlock its secrets, to peer into its dark corners. Dreams of being locked out of rooms show us that an examination of the unconscious is in progress—but that we are not yet ready to open the door.

▲ Dreaming of looking down on a house could indicate that you have gained insight into your psyche.

STAIRWAYS

Stairways are a common metaphor for advancement (or otherwise), ambition, and progress in life. Walking down to a cellar indicates delving deeper into the unconscious, while walking up to an attic suggests a focus on cerebral matters.

Travel

MAPS AND PASSPORTS

▲ A familiar map implies you have the knowledge to navigate a situation.

In our waking life we look at maps when we are trying to figure out how to get where we want to go. A map in a dream can carry the same meaning: It signifies that you are working out how to achieve a goal, or that you are considering taking a new direction in life. A map is a clear symbol of discovery and can relate to the journey of self-discovery we take into the psyche within our dreams. Is the map showing familiar or uncharted territory? Is it complete or missing something? Your dream could be telling you that you need to look deeper or go further.

POSITIVE INTERPRETATION

Finding a map easy to follow indicates that you are on the right path toward some goal. Does the map show a place that you know or wish to go to, or is it of some kind of magical land? You may notice, or remember, that the map of your dream differs from the cartography of that place in waking life. If so, consider those differences: They probably contain a clue to the deeper meaning of your dream.

NEGATIVE INTERPRETATION

If the map in your dream is hard to read, this implies that you are unsure how to get out of current difficulties. An indecipherable map can mean that you have lost your way, or that you are unhappy with your current circumstances.

GLOBES

Spheres generally signify a complete view from all angles. A globe can be a highly positive sign that you are considering a wider, more global perspective, or that you feel in control: A globe allows you to hold the world in your hand.

PASSPORTS

A symbol of identity, a passport can relate to feelings of belonging or acceptability. One needs a passport to pass through borders of foreign countries, so a dream concerning this documentation can suggest that you feel you have the right to pass into a new stage of life. It could also mean that your unconscious is giving you the go-ahead to explore (or face) some newly uncovered aspect of your personality.

TREASURE MAPS

A map that shows where treasure is points toward being on the verge of uncovering (or accepting) something beautiful and worthwhile—perhaps part of ourselves. The letter "X" is commonly used to mark the spot, so an "X" painted on any dream object can also indicate this.

◀ Travel dreams are usually about our journey through life. Are you the passenger or the one in control?

LUGGAGE

▲ More luggage than you can carry suggests it is time to let some things go.

In the dream world, luggage can symbolize preparations or the resources that we have at our disposal. It is also a metaphor for the mental and emotional baggage we carry with us on the journey of life, which may stem from our past history or our current commitments. The weight of our bags and how easily we carry them in the dream indicates our attitude toward our emotional commitments or burdens we carry.

POSITIVE INTERPRETATION

Feeling that you are traveling light or have everything you need for a journey is a reassuring and positive dream. If someone else is carrying the luggage, this suggests that you have support to aid you in an emotional difficulty. Some dream analysts believe that, for a woman, a suitcase or bag can also represent the womb and thus issues concerning childbearing; others interpret luggage as a yonic symbol—that is, representing female sexuality.

NEGATIVE INTERPRETATION

If the bags in your dream are heavy, large, or cumbersome this signifies that you feel burdened by the emotional demands on you, or perhaps weighed down by past issues. Is it time to put the bags down and move on without them? Unpacking bags suggests that you are ready to free yourself of some emotional issue or a difficult relationship or job.

WALLETS AND PURSES

Containing everything we need for our day-to-day needs, such as money and identifying documents, as well as multiple personal items, wallets and purses represent your ability to manage on a day-to-day level. They can also symbolize your identity.

LOSING A WALLET OR BAG

This dream scenario suggests personal anxieties. It's a common dream when you are in a transitional stage of life—leaving home for the first time, having your children leave home, or a relationship break-up, for example. In your dream, does the purse contain some specific item? If so, think what that object might signify.

PACKING

Dreams about packing luggage may intimate that you are gathering everything you need for an important event. If you are putting something in a suitcase and hiding it away, this could point to unpleasant feelings or a traumatic memory that is best left undisturbed.

ROADS

▲ Dreaming that you find a clear path through a forest is a highly positive sign.

A road naturally represents the path we travel in our life's journey and, more specifically, the direction you are currently taking. Is the surface of the road smooth or marked with potholes? Is it winding or straight, going uphill or downhill? The type of road and your progress along it is significant, as are any road signs that you pass or other features that you see. The destination is also meaningful: Do you know where you are headed in the dream, or does the road seem to stretch into nothingness or end in a dead end?

POSITIVE INTERPRETATION

A smooth road, or a freeway, shows that you are making fast progress toward a particular goal, or that generally all is going well in your life (unless you are speeding along too fast). A clear sense of destination is also a positive sign. Traveling at speed downhill could indicate freedom, but could also suggest that life is on a downward path; similarly an uphill road can indicate struggle, or alternatively could be a sense of moving onward and upward. Look to other aspects of the dream and any emotions you experience within it for further clues.

NEGATIVE INTERPRETATION

Winding roads reveal that you are taking an overly long and complicated approach to something. Obstacles in the road or stop signs could refer to difficulties you are facing, or may be a message that you are going along a path that is likely to cause problems in the future. Always pay attention to any written signs that you come across in your dream, as these often carry a significant message.

CROSSROAD OR FORK IN THE ROAD

You are at a point in your life when you need to make a decision about the direction you wish to go in. Does one road seem more appealing than another? If two roads merge into one, this can indicate union—a partnership, or perhaps the successful union of two distinct parts of your psyche.

BRIDGES

Bridges close gaps and are crossing points (often over water, which signifies emotion). There is a sense of moving from one terrain—or stage of life—to the next and in this way they serve as a metaphor for transition.

LABYRINTHS

A labyrinth or maze is a convoluted pathway to a central point and represents confusion. It is also a common symbol of spiritual endeavor and symbolizes life itself, as well as the virtue of patience.

CARS

Cars in dreams often represent the self, and the act of driving is our ability to control a situation. In any dream of being in a vehicle, the role we have been cast in matters. Are you the driver of the vehicle or a passenger with no control over where you are going? Some authorities believe that the car is a metaphor for the male sexual drive, and on a wider level the drive to succeed and achieve for both men and women. The color of the car may point toward a particular aspect of yourself or current concerns *(see Colors, pages 132–141)*.

POSITIVE INTERPRETATION

If you are driving along an open road, this represents freedom and the ability to travel your own path in life. Driving a new or unfamiliar car may reflect a new role that you are taking on in life. If you are driving a car that is powerful or a status symbol then this can signify feelings of effectiveness and strength. Overtaking can be a reference to competing with others.

NEGATIVE INTERPRETATION

A vehicle in a poor state of repair points to feeling incapable of reaching your destination; if the brakes fail, this suggests a fear that you are in a situation that you cannot control. Driving a cheap car could indicate you lack the resources you need to achieve a life aim, while obstacles in your pathway are a clear metaphor for things that are blocking or sabotaging progress.

SERVICE STATIONS

Running out of gas or filling up at a service station can reflect your energy levels in life. Are you running on empty and do you need to refuel? A gas hose can serve as a phallic metaphor, and as an extension, the act of refueling a car can be a veiled reference to sex.

TRAFFIC JAMS

A traffic jam represents the helpless feeling of being part of the herd: It signifies that you are traveling the same way as others without being able to change direction. Does your car escape the crush by some fantastic means? If so, this is your unconscious self encouraging you to find a means to break away.

EMERGENCY STOP

A vehicle coming to a sudden stop could be a warning from the unconscious that you should put the brakes on a project or situation. Give some thought to the dream event that brings about the stop: Were you about to drive off a precipice? If you stopped to avoid hitting a pedestrian, who was that person? What might he or she signify?

BACKSEAT DRIVER

Taking directions from a passenger in the car can signify either helpful advice or—more usually—unwelcome interference in your life. The person directing may represent an aspect of yourself that wants more of a say in the decisions you are currently making.

DRIVING SOMEONE ELSE'S CAR

If in your dream you are uneasy driving a car that is not your own, this suggests that you feel your decisions are being overly influenced by another person—or perhaps the part of your psyche that this person represents.

CRASHING A CAR

Crashing or wrecking a vehicle symbolizes conflict or chaos; a head-on crash with another car means you are on a collision course with someone in waking life.

WORKING VEHICLES

If your dream focuses on a vehicle such as bulldozer or snowplow, then this indicates that you are tough enough to push obstacles out of your way by sheer force of will.

▲ Driving a racing car suggests swift progress—so long as you feel in control.

PUBLIC TRANSPORT

▲ Railway bridges represent transition, one that you are sharing with others.

While a private vehicle, such as a car, often represents the self, a public vehicle, such as a bus or a train, can symbolize the part of us that identifies as a member of a group. Dreams that involve buses or trains generally refer to goals or situations that we undertake with others, perhaps relating to work or some other shared endeavor. It can also refer to the community to which we belong.

POSITIVE INTERPRETATION

Traveling by public vehicle can suggest a sense of belonging and cooperation. If you are driving, this suggests that you are leading—or feel responsible for—a group of people, such as a family or a work team, and perhaps ably steering them to a harmonious outcome or destination. Consider who is in the bus with you?

NEGATIVE INTERPRETATION

Being on a speeding train or bus can be thrilling, or terrifying, so your emotions in the dream are the best indication of what this means. A very slow bus or train journey suggests that you are being held back or that a life situation is taking too long to resolve itself. If you dream of a freight train, this can point to issues or burdens that you are carrying along your life journey. The type of freight may also be relevant.

TUNNELS

Entering a tunnel symbolizes traveling into the darkness—an unknown situation from which you cannot escape. This could be a reference to an emotional difficulty, such as depression, or it could be a reminder that patience is needed and you will come out the other side into the light again. Some dream analysts interpret this dream as a reference to sexual intercourse.

A DERAILED TRAIN

A train that has come off the tracks means that something in waking life has changed and cannot easily be reverted. Perhaps your unconscious is advising you to do whatever it takes to change direction, without regard to the wreckage that might result?

BUS OR TRAIN STATION

A terminus is a clear indication that no further progress can be made, whereas getting on a train suggests embarking on a new adventure or stage of life. If you cannot decide which train to get, this reflects uncertainty about which direction to take in life.

BOATS

▲ Rowing requires strength and stamina; your dream may be urging you on.

Dreams of boats, or being in boats, are often positive: They suggest you are successfully navigating emotional waters. Many cultures include the concept of crossing water with the help of a ferryman as we transition from life to death. This meaning may be reflected in your dream, particularly if you dream that you are being taken from one shore to another. Boats can also reflect transitional situations, moving from one stage of life to another. The safety of the vessel, the turbulence or otherwise of the water, and the speed at which you are traveling are all likely to be significant.

POSITIVE INTERPRETATION

If the sun is shining and the water is calm, this is a happy dream that reflects a sense that you are traveling in the right direction. Seeing the horizon in the distance suggests optimism about the future.

NEGATIVE INTERPRETATION

If the boat in your dream is sinking or the seas are stormy, this suggests you are feeling anxious about a situation becoming overwhelming and fear that you will be unable to cope or are "drowning" in an emotion. A boat that is in a state of disrepair reflects a lack of confidence about your ability to navigate your situation.

DISEMBARKING

Alighting from a boat can be a hazardous undertaking. It means moving from one element (water) to another (dry land). Since bodies of water often represent the truths hidden in the unconscious mind, this might represent a kind of retreat: Is there something that you are unwilling to face?

ROWING

Using oars in a boat suggests that you are delving below the surface of your psyche and breaking through to a greater emotional understanding. But rowing is harder work than it looks, so your dream may be a call to put the effort in if you are to make progress.

DRIFTING

If the boat is drifting across the water, this implies you are lacking direction and drifting in your life. If the boat is anchored, then this indicates feelings of security and belonging, particularly in your home or relationships.

TRAVEL

AIRPLANES

▲ Airplanes represent daring—this dream may be encouraging risk taking.

Flying an aircraft in a dream can represent a sense of liberation, but much depends on the dream experience. Are you the pilot confidently navigating the skies or terrified that your lack of expertise will cause you to crash? If you are high above the clouds in your dream this implies some kind of spiritual breakthrough, while hovering near the ground may suggest that something is holding you back in waking life. (*See Flying, page 50.*)

POSITIVE INTERPRETATION

Plane dreams can concern freedom and new opportunity. Taking to the air can show that a new project or life stage is about to take off in your life, while landing can indicate that you are ready to integrate new understanding into your daily life, or that a project or idea is about to make solid progress (and is on "firm ground").

NEGATIVE INTERPRETATION

Being grounded in a plane is a metaphor for feelings of stagnation and lack of progress. A circling plane that is unable to land suggests you are going round and round in your waking life, again making little progress. If you are on the ground under attack from a plane or from bombs being dropped, this reveals a fear of some disaster that you cannot protect yourself from.

PLANE CRASHES

This dream scenario can reflect an actual fear of flying, especially if you have a trip coming up. Otherwise, it may indicate a foreboding that something is going to come crashing down in your life—perhaps a precarious situation is no longer sustainable.

PARACHUTES

A parachute provides a way out of a dangerous situation, so that you can save yourself; it is also a symbol of forethought and protection. In a dream, this object could be a warning that you need to take precautionary measures to avoid leaving yourself vulnerable, or perhaps it is an indication that there is an unusual way out of a current problem.

AIRPORTS

An airport is a place of arrivals and departures, of meetings and separations. As such it can symbolize births and deaths—or other forms of beginning and ending.

MISSING A FLIGHT, TRAIN, OR BUS

▲ Time pressure could suggest a feeling that the clock is ticking.

This common anxiety dream often reflects a waking fear of missing an important deadline or appointment, or perhaps failing an exam *(see also Being Tested, page 56)*. More generally, missing a connection on a journey could reveal a feeling that an opportunity has passed you by, or that something that seemed to have potential is no longer open to you, perhaps through your own hesitancy or inefficiency.

POSITIVE INTERPRETATION

A dream of a missed connection could be a reminder to stop delaying and commit to an opportunity by taking the first steps toward it. If you feel happy to have missed a form of transport, this suggests that you have managed to avoid some undesirable situation.

NEGATIVE INTERPRETATION

It is important to look at what has caused you to miss the flight—if it is your own fault, then this could be recognition that you have done something to sabotage your progress in real life. If there has been some mishap or obstruction, this probably represents the issue, person, or the aspect of yourself that you blame for the lost opportunity.

LOST TICKETS

If you have lost your ticket or are prevented from boarding by an authority figure, this suggests a sense of inadequacy or unworthiness. Lost tickets or missing luggage could also be an acknowledgment that you are not sufficiently prepared for an opportunity. *(See Maps and Passports, page 73.)*

CONNECTING TRANSPORT

When a journey goes awry—especially if you are left behind when others travel onward—this could point to some emotional disconnection in your waking life. Perhaps you and a partner have become disconnected or are headed in different directions.

WATCHING THE TRANSPORTATION LEAVE

If you can see the plane or train leaving, this could suggest that you are closer than you think to achieving your aim. But if the transportation is long gone, then you are pointlessly hankering for something no longer within your reach.

Everyday Items

CONTAINERS

▲ The legend of Pandora could refer to the destructive desires we hold within.

Containers can mean a multitude of things within the dream context. Boxes, lidded caskets, and chests all represent some kind of secret that it may be unwise to reveal. Many ancient myths centered around this idea, such as the tale of Pandora who opened a box and released all the woes of the world. The kind of container you dream about is significant, as is what you find inside it. Opening a chest that contains gold or precious stones is a very different dream than one in which you find a nest of snakes inside.

POSITIVE INTERPRETATION

We all fantasize about finding a chest filled with treasure. When this image appears in your dreams, it can mean finding hidden talents within or uncovering new opportunities. If you dream of putting things safely in a box, your unconscious could be suggesting that you do not seek to open up about a certain aspect of your psyche, but would rather leave it undisturbed.

NEGATIVE INTERPRETATION

A broken or damaged container shows that something has been exposed or revealed against our will. But there is a saying that "there is a crack in everything; it's how the light gets in." Sometimes a damaged pot can be a thing of beauty. In China, repaired containers such as tea bowls are highly prized—because they have visible character and history.

CUPS AND CHALICES

These are often yonic symbols—representations of female sexuality. Drinking from a cup may represent the act of offering oneself to another (if you are a woman), either sexually or in some other way. It can also symbolize drinking deeply from life's experience. What is in the cup can sometimes be more significant than the vessel.

COOKING POTS

In ancient times, a pot was a treasured possession because it enabled you to cook over a fire. In dreams, it is a symbol of sustenance, both physical and spiritual, and also family (gathering around the pot). Another meaning is fertility and pregnancy.

LIDS

Putting the lid on a pot or container can either symbolize covering something up or keeping it safely contained. Sometimes a lid may represent the eyelid, which is a means of averting the gaze from something unpleasant—perhaps an unpalatable truth?

◀ The simplest household item can be redolent of our personal histories, but can also have wider dream meanings.

MONEY

▲ We dream of being rich in our waking life, because money creates possibilities.

Money is highly significant in our waking life, and so it is not surprising that it often turns up in our dreams, too. It is the great facilitator, enabling us to buy the things we want, go to the places we are interested in, enjoy activities, and treat ourselves. It is also a status symbol as being successful generally equates to having a lot of money. Gifts of money reflect emotional generosity and a feeling that you have more than enough in life. If you are struggling to give money in a dream, that could point to some emotional blockage that needs your attention.

POSITIVE INTERPRETATION

Dreaming of finding money or having a lot of money can be a clear sign of abundance or satisfaction. It can symbolize spiritual or emotional riches as well as material wealth. Money also represents security, so dreaming you have enough can mean you feel secure in your life or a relationship.

NEGATIVE INTERPRETATION

Losing money reflects insecurity or concern about losing status; if you don't have the money to pay an admission fee, this can relate to feelings of exclusion or lack of progress. Hoarding money is also about insecurity, and a miser could represent someone who takes more than they give. A lack of funds can also relate to your energy levels—perhaps you do not have enough for the current demands on you.

BANKS

Making a deposit symbolizes storing up resources (energy) for the future; withdrawing money can represent drawing on your inner reserves. A bank is a place where exchanges (giving and taking) occur. Does this resonate when thinking about your dream?

COINS AND BANKNOTES

Coins are made from metal, which has always had a value to humankind, and represent good fortune (as in a "lucky coin"). As a circle they also symbolize the circle of life or completion. Sometimes the design on a coin may have significance: A shield, crown, or a head, for example. Think about what these symbols mean to you. Paper banknotes can represent a promise—is the note torn or broken?

INHERITANCE

Inheriting money points to the reaping of benefits, to the idea that previous groundwork is now paying dividends. This groundwork may be study, hard work, or investment in any sense of the word.

JEWELRY

▲ Jewelry is used for adornment, and to both store and show off wealth.

Jewels represent status and wealth, but jewelry also allows you to beautify yourself for public display. The stones are dug up from the ground—the deepest regions of the earth—and then have to be worked on to turn them into something that is presentable and fit to be displayed. In this way jewelry can be a symbol for our own psyche, which is a work in progress. Jewelry is often worn for special occasions, so a specific piece of jewelry could be a metaphor for these events or for a particular person.

POSITIVE INTERPRETATION

Beautiful sparkling jewelry reflects feeling good about yourself. Being given jewelry implies you feel recognized or appreciated in your waking life, or that you have found some hidden treasure (such as spiritual or religious understanding). A particular item of jewelry, such as a necklace or bracelet, could be your unconscious mind drawing your attention to that part of the body (see The Human Body, pages 32–45).

NEGATIVE INTERPRETATION

Losing a piece of jewelry in a dream implies you have lost something of value to you. Looking at someone else who has jewelry or gazing at jewelry locked in a cabinet can imply feelings of envy or worthlessness.

STONES

If the stone is your birthstone then this is likely to reflect you in your dream. A diamond is completely transparent and a symbol of clarity and understanding. The color of other stones may also be significant and should be taken into consideration (see Colors, pages 132–141). Cut stones are often multifaceted; is the dream suggesting you need to look at an issue from another angle?

RINGS

Rings can represent sexuality. As a circle, they also represent continuity and completion—one reason why the wedding ring is a symbol of commitment.

BROOCHES

Worn on the chest like a medal, a brooch can reflect feelings of pride. If another person fastens the brooch on you this may imply recognition from others, or perhaps that someone is trying to attach public blame to you. Your feelings about the brooch in the dream will direct you to the correct interpretation.

CLOTHING

In dreams, clothing can have much to reveal about the image we wish to portray to the outside world, and also what want to cover up. Clothes signal one's role or status—think of a monarch's robes or priest's vestments. They are the vehicle through which we express our affinity to a certain group of people, from punks to the high-fashion jet set, and they demonstrate our work, uniforms or the suits of business people. Clothes also serve to protect us, not only from cold and injury, but also shielding our vulnerabilities.

POSITIVE INTERPRETATION

New clothes are a metaphor for making a new start or changing the way you operate within the world. If you feel good about what you are wearing this indicates confidence. Clothes in particular colors may suggest a need for what that color represents (*see Colors, pages 132–141*).

NEGATIVE INTERPRETATION

Wearing many layers of clothing in a dream can mean seeking to hide oneself. Torn or dirty clothing can illustrate feelings of rebellion or nonconformity (as in the punk rock subculture), while tight clothes can suggest feeling restricted. It's common to dream of wearing inappropriate or inadequate clothing for an occasion, and this can reveal feelings of inadequacy or uncertainty.

HATS

A visual symbol for our ideas and opinions, putting a hat on or taking it off can mean a change of mind. Is it a hat you feel comfortable wearing? A hat can also be about the role you are performing in waking life. Hats or head coverings are often worn by authority figures.

UNDERWEAR

Dreams featuring underwear concern feelings about your sexuality or issues regarding sex. If the underwear is very revealing, or it is dirty, this could point to some anxiety regarding this area of your life.

SHOES AND BOOTS

In Freud's view, the act of putting on a shoe is a sexual image. Otherwise, shoes and boots can be about the direction you are moving in life. It matters whether you are comfortable (indicating you are at peace with the path you are taking) or uncomfortable (some inner turmoil with it).

COSTUME PARTY

This is often a desire to experiment with a completely new way of being. Pay attention to the nature of your costume—is it something you wore at some point in the past? If so, it might point to feelings experienced at this time that are resurfacing.

TROUSERS

Traditionally male attire can reflect masculine attitudes or one's masculine side. Like all forked things, trousers can point to a dilemma: If you are ironing one pant leg, this suggests your unconscious is prompting you to take one path (the smooth one) rather than the other.

UNIFORMS

The meaning will vary depending on the type of uniform and your attitude to it. Is it you wearing the uniform or someone else? If you feel uncomfortable in your uniform, or it is ill-fitting, then this suggests you are similarly uncomfortable with the role you are playing.

GLOVES

We wear gloves for dirty or dangerous tasks. They could signify hiding your actions, since burglars and other criminals wear gloves. Are you worried about some morally questionable action that you are considering? Or are they pointing toward some specific activity such as boxing (which relates to fighting) or gardening (nurturing your inner self). The interpretation

▲ Dressing up allows us to adopt new roles. This 1868 illustration depicts revelers at a masquerade ball.

will depend of the type of glove worn. Gloves in a dream could also point to a fear of intimacy or contact.

TOOLS

▲ Dream objects are not bound by realism and may become supersized.

Tools are used to create, to access things, or to adapt raw materials into objects that are of use to us. In a dream, the questions to ask are always: What am I trying to transform or use? How does the tool work? And who is using or manipulating it? The tool may represent someone—including yourself—or some issue you are grappling with in real life. Are you trying to cut your way through, or dismantle something? The type of action performed by the tool may be significant.

POSITIVE INTERPRETATION

A dream in which a tool is being used might be showing you how to make the most of an opportunity, or indicating that you need to remove someone or something from a situation. There are phrases and sayings in all languages derived from our use of tools (we "hit the nail on the head" or "hammer a point home"), so think whether your dream is a visual symbol of such advice.

NEGATIVE INTERPRETATION

If you are using a tool ineptly or it is failing to work, this could represent something is going wrong in your waking life, or a feeling that you do not have the skills or resources to manage a task. Are you using the tool for the correct purpose or are you applying a tool intended for one thing to another (as in "using a sledgehammer to crack a nut")? This can be a sign that you are going about something in the wrong way.

CUTLERY

Spoons can signify nurture and satisfaction; forks and knives help reduce something to a manageable size and can also be weapons. The number of tines on a fork may signify a group, and a missing tine may represent a missing member of the group.

WORK TOOLS

Hammers and drills are often seen as phallic symbols, so in a dream context these tools may have a sexual meaning. Otherwise, they reflect a desire to break through or destroy some barrier of understanding in your waking life.

SHOVELS

This tool can denote hard work and industriousness. But it is also used to turn earth over, revealing something underneath or alternatively to cover something up. How is it being used in the dream, and what has been or is being buried?

WEAPONS

▲ This deity holds weapons and other objects, showing a multifaceted approach.

Weapons are the tools of attack—and of defense. In dreams these meanings can come to the fore, but we may be talking about inner conflict between warring sides of our personality or a power struggle between ourselves and someone else, rather than actual physical aggression. Many dream specialists agree with the Freudian theory that knives, daggers, guns, and swords symbolize the phallus and that their appearance in a dream may reflect male sexuality.

POSITIVE INTERPRETATION

Weapons serve as protection, and their appearance in a dream is usually a sign that you need to exercise caution or feel in danger in some way. But many weapons also serve as useful tools—Alexander the Great used his sword to cut through the impossible-to-unravel Gordian knot. Logical incisive (razor-sharp) thought can also be symbolized by cutting weapons. And weapons can represent strategic actions—it may be that you need to deploy these to achieve something in your waking life.

NEGATIVE INTERPRETATION

It is common to dream of attacking another person when we are consumed with repressed rage in real life, an example of a wish-fulfillment dream. Being stabbed in a dream indicates that you feel betrayed or injured by someone in real life. The part of the body that is injured is likely to be important (see *The Human Body, pages 32–45*).

BOW AND ARROW, AND GUNS

These weapons have the association of marksmanship and are fired from a safe distance. Where, and at whom, you are aiming the weapon can reveal how you feel about a goal in your waking life. The Roman god of desire, Cupid, shoots an arrow at someone to make him or her fall in love, and this meaning may also show up in your dream.

POISON

Poison is an indirect form of weaponry. When we are poisoned in a dream, some psychological injury is indicated—perhaps a situation has become toxic or our opinion of someone has been altered by unwelcome knowledge.

KNIVES AND SCISSORS

Knives are used for cutting, and can represent divisions (*see Cutlery, page 90*). Scissors have two blades and represent anything that needs to work together (a partnership, for example), as well as a cutting blade. Scissors are used to cut ties that bind us, so could reflect the necessary ending of a relationship.

EVERYDAY ITEMS

FOOD AND DRINK

A dream of food can be a straightforward wish-fulfillment dream, or it can mean that you are hungry (dreams about eating can help you to stay asleep in spite of hunger). But most often food dreams are about your emotional or spiritual well-being. Our first experiences of closeness and nurture as a baby are bound up with feeding, meaning that food is inextricably linked with love and care both in our waking lives and in our dreams.

POSITIVE INTERPRETATION

Happy eating and drinking dreams indicate you feel nurtured and satisfied, mentally and physically, in real life. Large amounts of food in a dream or a lavish banquet suggests abundance. This can—by extension—mean fertility or success, assuming you have access to, and feel positive toward, the banquet.

NEGATIVE INTERPRETATION

If someone you know serves you food that is off or spoiled in a dream, perhaps this person is not serving you well in real life. If he or she is your parent this can be a reflection of a childhood in which you were not fully nurtured. Forcing yourself to eat something you dislike or that is bad for you is often a sign that you are in some unpalatable situation. Having food taken away from you is a sign of lost opportunities, being blocked, or disrespected.

WINE

Wine or other alcohol flows freely at many celebrations and in a dream can symbolize success or achievements. However, your attitude to alcohol in real life is likely to be significant. If you or someone close to you has addiction issues, or if you belong to a religion or belief system that disapproves of it, then wine can stand for negatives such as transgression or loss of self-control.

BREAKFAST

This meal is the breaking of our fast after the long sleep of the night. In a dream this can signify that some kind of drought or hiatus in your life is coming to an end and a new phase is about to begin.

EGGS

Eggs are a symbol of the circle of life. They can represent conception and birth of a child or an idea. Broken eggs can mean an ending of some potential event. Eggs are both strong, under certain pressures and circumstances, and fragile under others. This duality may speak to your own sense of yourself.

MEAT

If it is clear what animal you are eating in the dream then this could be a wish to take on that animal's characteristic—for example, if you find yourself eating lion meat, are you wanting to internalize courage or find it within?

APPETITE

Having an insatiable appetite or displaying greed in a dream reflects lack of satisfaction, or an anxiety that current good times will not last. Biting and chewing in a dream is a sensual pleasure, and thus is often said to represent the sexual act.

EATING WITH OTHERS

A convivial meal represents relationships and family—"breaking bread" with someone is a way to confirm a connection. Sharing food can represent sharing your ideas, feelings, or even your body (through sex).

▲ Food can be a metaphor for love, satisfaction, and fulfillment—or lack, greed, and decay. No wonder artists such as Van Dyck made studies of it.

FURNITURE

▲ Tables symbolize togetherness; sitting alone indicates separation or loneliness.

A house in a dream is most commonly a symbol of the self or the mind. It follows that the people and things that fill the house symbolize the thoughts and attitudes that crowd our minds. Some of them are permanent fixtures, others come and go. Furniture in dreams can be metonymic—meaning it stands for the activity with which it is associated. Thus your bed could imply sex or rest; your boss's chair might symbolize authority or concerns about your career; and your kitchen table could represent the family dynamic.

POSITIVE INTERPRETATION

If you are arranging furniture and putting everything in its correct place, this suggests you are organizing your thoughts or life in a new or better way. New furniture represents new ideas—are you getting rid of old or damaged furniture (outdated or inherited ideas)? Look at your associations with the things you are throwing out: Do they remind you of a particular time or person in your life?

NEGATIVE INTERPRETATION

If there is too much furniture in a room or home, could it be that your mind is similarly overcrowded? Dark and ugly furniture could be a metaphor for negative thoughts taking up too much room in your mind. Is the furniture hiding something? A closed closet or a locked drawer is a clear symbol of secrecy (*see Containers, page 85*) while carpets, curtains, and throws are used to cover things up.

BEDS

A bed is where we sleep and rest, where we are intimate with our partner, where we conceive our children, where we go when we are ill or troubled, and (often) where we die. Any one of these functions may be relevant to a dream in which the bed is significant.

TABLES

Tables indicate community and connectedness. Where you are sitting at the table can reflect your social standing.

CHAIRS

A chair can represent short-term passivity, perhaps you are sitting out a difficult time. It can also represent taking a seat at a discussion, and some chairs are reserved for those in authority. This four-legged small piece of furniture could also be a stylized image of a crawling baby (perhaps representing your own self).

LIGHTS, CANDLES, AND TORCHES

▲ Florence Nightingale, the Lady of the Lamp, brought hope to the wounded.

Light in any form is likely to represent metaphorical forms of illumination, such as a dawning awareness, enlightenment, or a flicker of insight. You should certainly consider the nature of the light: Is it a powerful beam from a searchlight, a guttering candle, or a dim and naked bulb? These forms of light will all contain clues that you should explore. But generally light is a positive dream image, standing for guidance, hope, and clarity.

POSITIVE INTERPRETATION

Dreaming of switching a light on could be the renewal of optimism in a dark situation, or a belief that a new insight may change the outcome. We are guided by light, so they also represent anyone who serves as a mentor to you. This is particularly relevant if the light is one specifically intended for guidance, such as the lamp of a lighthouse.

NEGATIVE INTERPRETATION

Switching off a light may reflect a feeling that a current situation is hopeless. Since light is associated with life, a dimmed light can suggest illness or the loss of loved one (as can a snuffed-out candle, see right). Stumbling around in the dark can be a clear sign that you feel a lack of guidance.

FLASHLIGHTS

If you are using a bright light to guide you through the dark, this can illustrate that you are prepared to face the darkness of the soul and reach greater clarity. Flaming torches have a similar meaning.

MATCHES

A match gives light very briefly and is used to start a fire. Dream matches can indicate the small opportunities you have to begin something bigger.

CANDLES

A candle can have many meanings. Its shape means it can be a phallic symbol; but more commonly it represents hope, continuity, and (because one candle lights the next) connectivity. Candles are often used in religious ceremonies and are lit to commemorate a loved one, so can represent the flame of life itself.

HOUSEHOLD OBJECTS

Dreams are not stage sets—nothing that appears in your dream is merely scenery. If you dream of an item, however ordinary, be aware that it is there for a reason and its function is to tell you something. The objects we use in everyday life are inevitably personal and can carry a highly individual message: If you use a particular book as a doorstop, for example, then that book may represent the means of keeping some door of opportunity open. And consider if there is anyone you associate with a particular item—a pipe may bring to mind your grandfather, while a paintbrush could suggest a particular friend.

POSITIVE INTERPRETATION

Think about the function of the object you dreamt of, as this can reveal how your mind is encouraging you to act. For example, items that have a lens (such as spectacles or a telescope), a screen (such as a computer), or a reflection (such as a mirror) could all be suggesting you take a closer look at something. A magical or beautiful object may be showing you a new solution. Toys and other childhood belongings indicate a general wish to go back to a time of greater innocence.

NEGATIVE INTERPRETATION

A garbage can or bag is an illustration of something that is unwanted and needs to be thrown out. What is being dumped and what does this item relate to in your life? In dreams, everyday items can be chimerical—and sometimes in nightmarish ways: A loaf of bread turns out to be a severed head, a tree is not a tree but a man-eating troll… These frightening revelations point to your deepest fears.

BROOMS

Are you sweeping away old ideas or the debris of the past to create a clean space for new ideas? Think about the room or area in which you are sweeping and what the broom is removing, as these are important clues as to the broom's significance and meaning.

UMBRELLAS

Taking an umbrella with you in case of rain is a precautionary action, and umbrellas in dreams can symbolize the emotional steps we take to protect ourselves from changes in our situation. But umbrellas also function as parasols, guarding against sun as well as rain. Does the umbrella of your dream represent some dual, contradictory function?

MIRRORS

Mirror, mirror on the wall… Mirrors in dreams imply you are looking deeply into aspects of yourself. Think about what your reflection shows: It could be revealing an obscure aspect of your psyche. Being happy with your reflection suggests self-acceptance, while feeling ugly or looking into a broken mirror points toward self-rejection or low self-esteem.

MUSICAL INSTRUMENTS

If you dream of an instrument you play, then this dream is likely to be a form of mental rehearsal. Music is an expression of emotion and so the type of sound you are producing can be a sign of your emotional well-being. Is it harmonious or discordant? Different instruments can represent parts of the self. Curvaceous violins and cellos often stand for the womanly form or female; trumpets and trombones can be phallic symbols; pianos have many keys, which can represent revelations and solutions.

LETTERS AND BOOKS

Letters and books usually draw the dreamer's attention to an important message or intuition; books are a repository of knowledge. Opening an envelope demonstrates a willingness to listen, while leaving the envelope sealed means you are missing something.

ELECTRONIC ITEMS

If you dream of something playing on a TV, it is likely to be a scenario from your own life, one

▲ A parasol protects from the hot sun; this symbol suggests a worry that a situation may become harmful.

that is easier to look at from a distance. A remote control may represent a desire to have greater influence over how something is playing out. A blank TV screen symbolizes a situation you are choosing not to look at.

Nature

MOUNTAINS
AND HILLS

▲ Mountains have spiritual significance, as they soar from Earth to the heavens.

Mountains are symbols of challenge and aspiration. A dream that you are climbing a mountain is very likely to be connected to a desire to reach some higher plane—in your career or your spiritual journey, or in some other aspect of life. Valleys are usually places of ease and plenty, green oases in the mountainous uplands, and they often represent rest and recuperation. Dreaming you are on a peak, looking over a mountain range is often a dream metaphor for the course of a life, with all its ups and downs. Are you looking back (to the past) or ahead (to the future)?

POSITIVE INTERPRETATION

We often describe success or victory in terms that make metaphorical reference to mountains. We speak of someone being "at their peak" or of "reaching the top." If you dream of conquering a mountain, then that is a clear indication of an ambitious attitude. If you are on top, what can you see? The view may be giving you a wider perspective on aspects of your journey.

NEGATIVE INTERPRETATION

If your dream features an arduous uphill slog, that points to a struggle to make progress in your waking life. Look to the details of the dream to see if the unconscious is hinting at a way to resolve the problem. Does assistance come in your dream? What form does it take?

NAMED MOUNTAINS

A mountain's name can point to your dream's meaning. If your dream includes a specific peak or range, consider any puns or wordplay that could be contained within that name.

CLIFFS OR CLIFFTOPS

To dream of a cliff edge is to know that there is a looming danger. Climbing without safety gear could be a message that you are taking unnecessary risks.

VOLCANOES

A dream volcano can elude to the bursting forth of repressed emotion in your waking life. Are you about to erupt, or is someone else?

◀ A landscape may appear to be merely the backdrop to the action in our dreams, but it is always significant.

LANDSCAPES

Open landscapes are common features of dreams. The nature of the terrain can often serve as an indication of the kinds of difficulties or problems that the unconscious mind fears or is trying to bring to the attention of the consciousness. Pay attention to whether you are alone in the wild open space that your dreaming self has created, and how you feel: This can reveal your deepest emotions about your present state.

POSITIVE INTERPRETATION

If you feel safe and happy in the landscape, that is a good sign. It is also positive if your dream has set you a goal or given you a sense of purpose: Are you headed toward some emerald city of your own imagining? Do you get there in your dream, either by yourself or with help? Both scenarios are positive, but ask yourself what the help or helper might stand for.

NEGATIVE INTERPRETATION

Wilderness scenes can stand for desolation, for loneliness, and a sense of being deprived. In the dream the deprivation may be physical—a shortage of water or the absence of shelter—but these are usually metaphors for some spiritual or emotional lack. If you feel lost or have no idea where you are headed, this could indicate a lack of direction in your waking life.

A BEACH

Beaches represent the boundary between the known and the unknown, the relative comfort of the conscious on the one hand and the great boundless ocean of the unconscious mind on the other. If you are paddling in the shallows, that might suggest that you have not yet taken the plunge that is required of you. Are you being urged to dive in and find out what lies beneath the surface?

A BACKYARD

A backyard often represents your inner life: It is a circumscribed place in which nature has been tamed. A garden that is wild and in need of work suggests aspects of your personality need to be brought under control. A garden can also be a metaphor for a woman's sexual organs.

A SANDY DESERT

If you dream of a boundless sandy desert, then you are unconsciously acknowledging that change is happening around or within you. The sands can shift, dunes can move and change their shape overnight; the nights themselves can be as cold as the days are hot. In your dream, are you the master of this moving landscape, or are you at the mercy of this parched and unforgiving place?

A ROCKY PLACE

A rock-strewn wilderness can indicate a mass of difficulties that make life hard going. You may be "stuck between a rock and a hard place," as the saying goes: It may seem that all courses of action are as helpless as each other. Look to your dream to see from which direction help might come.

A CAVE

A dream of being in a cave implies a desire to withdraw from social contact. The cave is your protection, your shell, the place where you can be yourself without inhibition or outside judgment. If you share the cave with someone else, that

character could represent some aspect of your psyche that is trying to get through to you.

AN ISLAND

Dreaming you are alone on a desert island could suggest you are feeling self-sufficient and content with your own circumscribed world. Since an island is surrounded by water (which represents emotions), it can demonstrate feelings of isolation or an unwillingness to

▲ In a desert everything is constantly shifting, and it is essential to have the resources you need to survive.

engage with either your own feelings or with other people. Are you trying to get off the island, or are you using it as a refuge? How you feel about being on the island is significant.

FORESTS AND TREES

▲ Rosseau's lush jungle conjures up the magical primal qualities of the unknown.

Trees have a rich symbolism attached to them; longer lived than any human, they stand for posterity. It is often pointed out that many trees have root systems that are as extensive as the trunk and canopy we see above ground—and this is one of many graphic ways our dreaming mind presents to us the "visible" conscious and its counterpart, the invisible unconscious. A dream of a walk in the woods can be telling: Is there a path through the trees? Does your dreaming self know where it is headed? Are you somehow failing to "see the forest for the trees"?

POSITIVE INTERPRETATION

A dream forest can be a place of safety and also an image of community—a forest is itself a community of trees. What kind of forest features in your dream? Is it thriving? Does it have a name? Forests were also the protective home of our most distant tree-dwelling ancestors, and in more recent periods, they have served as hideouts during times of trouble (think of the legend of Robin Hood and his merry men in Sherwood Forest, England). These associations can make themselves felt in our dreams.

NEGATIVE INTERPRETATION

Forests can also stand for the darker recesses of the unconscious mind, the primal urges and the uncensored desires that Freud called the "id." It is no coincidence that in fairy tales forests are often filled with danger and wild beasts.

PLANTING A TREE OR FOREST

Planting trees can signal investment in the future, a long-term project. Trees already full of fruit suggest a plan is coming to fruition. (*See Fruit, pages 104–105.*)

CHOPPING DOWN TREES

Are you cutting yourself off from a family member or other deep-rooted connection, or mourning a loss of one? Sometimes this apparently destructive act might be positive, since logging is the first step in many a grand undertaking such a building a home.

THE NAMES OF TREES

The unconscious often uses imagery in dreams to generate visual puns. Consider what symbolism could be contained in wordplay: This could be in the name of the tree species or the part of the tree prominent in your dream.

FLOWERS
AND PLANTS

▲ Sunflowers—here by Van Gogh—are a symbol of warmth, hope, and happiness.

Flowers are symbols of impermanence, particularly the short-lived nature of beauty. In dreams, they serve to remind us that all things come to an end, however brightly they may bloom in their heyday. Many flowers are endowed by tradition with specific meanings—red roses for romance, white lilies for mourning—and these senses can transfer to our dream life. Flowers also traditionally represent femininity; the word "flower" is sometimes used to allude to the female genitals, so this could be another possible dream meaning to consider.

POSITIVE INTERPRETATION

Flowers are often presented as gifts. If someone gives you a flower in a dream, think which of your own gifts (talents) your unconscious mind could be drawing your attention to, or what the message behind the gift is. The identity of the giver might be as significant as the species of flower. Fields of plants or flowers may hint at growth or the flowering of an idea or business.

NEGATIVE INTERPRETATION

Dreams of weeds, overgrown gardens, or impenetrable foliage point toward an apparently inescapable situation or a bind that needs to be cleared, while thorns represent obstacles or the downside of a positive situation. Sometimes the solution is just to hack away—like the fairy-tale prince who chops through the brambles to reach his sleeping beauty. Dead or dying flowers could represent the death of a relationship.

A BOUQUET OR WREATH

A bouquet—a wreath, too—can be a token of victory or a symbol of loss and bereavement.

PARTICULAR FLOWERS

Poppies are associated with rest and sleep, because some species have a soporific effect. In the West, poppies are strongly linked with remembrance and war as they were one of the few flowers to grow on the battlefields and their red shade is the same color as the blood spilled there. Roses represent love. A pansy takes its name from the French word *pensée*—a thought—so wild pansies might stand for your own untamed thoughts. A daffodil is also known as a narcissus—from the Greek myth of a beautiful youth who was obsessed with his own reflection; are you too focused on yourself?

PLANT NAMES

Many plants have names that also serve as the given names of people. If you dream of roses or a laurel tree or heather, does someone you know have that name? What qualities do you associate with that person?

FRUIT

Fruit can be an image of development and growth, and also of family. Both descendants and ancestors are, so to speak, the fruit on our family tree, and our offspring are said to be "the fruit of our loins." But in dreams much depends on the particular fruit and the associations that we have with it. For example, if you find yourself in a dream enjoying a fruit that you hate in real life, that may be an indication that you should take a course of action that you have been hesitant to follow and it may turn out well.

POSITIVE INTERPRETATION

Fruit is the most ancient form of nourishment: Our prehuman ancestors ate fruit for eons before they discovered other foods, such as dairy and meat. Our unconscious mind knows this and associates fruit with sustenance, abundance, and also with sensual pleasure—since ripe fruits (along with honey) were the only source of sweetness until very recent times in human history.

NEGATIVE INTERPRETATION

Fruit can also represent the unstoppable approach of consequences for past actions. The things that we do eventually bear fruit, and bad things bear bad fruit. This is something to consider if you feel negatively about the fruit that features in your dreams, or if it is spoiled or rotten.

APPLES

In the Western tradition, apples are strongly associated with sin and wrongdoing—because traditionally the apple is the fruit that Eve was tempted to pick in the Garden of Eden (though, in fact, the Bible does not specify the type of fruit). A dream of taking an apple might therefore indicate guilt. In contrast, it could also suggest good health, echoing the saying "an apple a day keeps the doctor away."

BANANAS

These are a very common phallic symbol, but bananas can suggest other things too. The banana skin is a proverbial cause of a slip-up. Is there some hazard you should be looking to avoid? Bananas can also suggest frenzy or chaos, as referenced in the phrase "going bananas."

GRAPES

These vine fruits often stand for some kind of transformation, because of the process—seen as almost magical by ancient cultures—by which they can be made into wine. Is there some area of your life where the ordinary might take on an extraordinary aspect?

PICKING FRUIT

To pick fruit is to harvest the results of one's own work, especially work that is long-term and requires careful husbandry. Is there a situation in your life where you are about to reap reward, or feel that you ought to?

SPOILED FRUIT

It is common to dream of biting into a piece of fruit and finding that it is rotten or infested with worms. This clear image of disappointment, often associated with disgust, might well hint at some troubling or unhealthy situation in your waking life.

FRUIT AND SEX

Fruit is ripe with the sexual symbolism that can crop up in dreams. The cherry stands for virginity and the loss of virginity. Figs in many cultures are associated with the genitalia, both male and female, as well as fertility (because of their many seeds). Other sexualized body parts are often described in terms of fruit: melons for breasts and pear-shaped or peachy buttocks. Our dreams can pluck any of these images from the great orchard of symbolic meanings.

▲ Luscious fruit and beautiful flowers are nature's gifts, and they denote growth and development.

SUN AND SKY

▲ The sun, rising each morning to herald a new day, represents power and hope.

In dreams and waking life, the sun represents power in all its forms and light in all its senses. Every primitive society worshipped a sky-god who was identified with the sun: The Babylonians had Shamash, the Persians looked to Mithras, the Egyptians to Ra. Even in Christianity, Jesus is called the Sun of Righteousness. The sun is traditionally associated with masculine power (the moon with feminine), while the wide open skies can be a metaphor for our expansive minds.

POSITIVE INTERPRETATION

Dreams of a bright sun in a clear sky could indicate a striving on the part of the dreamer toward a kind of enlightenment or wisdom. It could also suggest a yearning for power and control over one's own world, or a wish to bestow warm blessings on everyone within that world. A rising sun suggests the hope of a new day, start, or opportunity.

NEGATIVE INTERPRETATION

A setting sun could suggest the end of something, while getting too close to the sun might indicate overarching ambition or recklessness, as in the Greek myth of Icarus. He conquered the sky but strayed so close to the sun that the wax holding his feathers together melted, costing him his wings and his life. Dark skies can suggest a mind clouded with anxiety.

SOLAR ECLIPSE

If you dream of an eclipse, this may be an indication that you feel overshadowed or deprived of some essential source of strength. Sinister solar events—the sun falling from the sky or changing to some unnatural color—indicate some fear about the loss or failure of something central to your life.

CLOUDS

Black clouds can be a metaphor for unhappiness or depression. You should closely examine any cloud-image that your unconscious mind presents to you: Why that object, and why in a fleeting and short-lived form?

SUNBEAMS

If the sun's rays penetrate the clouds and create a beam of light that falls on the earth, that is a symbol of optimism and a picture of a blessing. A cheerful person is sometimes called a sunbeam.

STARS, THE MOON, AND PLANETS

▲ Humankind has always searched for patterns and meaning in the night sky.

Curious humans have long observed the stars, the planets, and the moon, and wondered if their shapes and courses have an effect on earthly affairs: That is the idea behind the ancient practice of astrology. This in turn led to all sorts of associations between heavenly objects, the gods they are associated with, and the attributes of those gods. This rich vein of symbolism is something that often manifests in our dream life.

POSITIVE INTERPRETATION

The moon is the feminine principle that complements the masculine sign of the sun; it represents creativity, fruitfulness, and intuition. Flying to the moon represents exploration. The planets in their orbits stand for harmony and stability; stars, meanwhile, are mystic symbols of aspiration, hope, and perfect love. The constellations are patterns that we impose on the random scattering of the stars. Might you, in waking life, be seeing patterns where there are none, or does the name of the constellation reveal something about your inner life?

NEGATIVE INTERPRETATION

Dreams of the stars and planets can sometimes suggest a dark inevitability: Something that is "written in the stars" cannot be avoided, and certain conjunctions of the planets signal doom. The moon has links with uncontrollable madness—as in the word "lunatic" (from the Latin for moon, *luna*) or the folktale of the werewolf, whose inner animal self is unleashed by the full moon.

THE DIVINE PLANETS

Each planet has mythic associations that can play out in dreams. Mercury is fickle and carries messages; Venus embodies the feminine and is the image of love; Mars is her aggressive counterpart—masculine and warlike; Jupiter represents dominance and protection; Saturn stands for order, but also dark brooding; Uranus embodies sociability; Neptune, extravagance and sophistication; Pluto, wealth.

STARRY SKIES

A sky filled with stars could signify an abundance of possibilities. Are you aiming for the stars in your dream, meaning you have high ambitions?

ASPECTS OF THE MOON

The ever-changing shape of the moon may be significant in a dream, as can the fact that it always keeps the same face to Earth. Is there some unseen dark side that your dream is pointing you toward? For women, the moon may also be a reference to the menstrual cycle or to fertility.

NATURE

ICE

▲ This snowy scene captures the harshness and the playfulness of winter.

Water often represents emotions in dreams, and since ice is frozen water, its main dream meaning is concerned with a drastic cooling of feeling. This may be an accurate portrayal of reality or just our waking perception. But ice is also an extremely versatile symbol because, like fire, it means many different things to us and it is inherently changeable. Dreams of ice should always be considered within the context of the other elements of the dream: The mood, the people who are there, and the events that occur.

POSITIVE INTERPRETATION

Ice is a slang term for diamonds and can be a symbol of wealth. But more commonly, ice represents some kind of freeze or halt—melting ice, by contrast, represents a thawing of attitudes of feelings. Is there some situation in your life where a rapprochement is desirable? Or perhaps it is time to activate a project that has been "put on ice."

NEGATIVE INTERPRETATION

Ice often signifies that you feel frozen or numbed in some emotional or sexual way; your unconscious mind may be advising you to warm up. It might also mean that you cannot access something that belongs to you (as in "frozen assets").

ICEBERGS

Icebergs proverbially hide most of themselves beneath the surface—and so are a perfect picture of the relationship between the conscious and the unconscious mind. Consider what is happening to the iceberg in your dream.

ARCTIC LANDSCAPES

The cold Arctic and Antarctic are our world's extremities, both in terms of their geographical position and of the harsh conditions. These landscapes could suggest that you are exploring some extreme aspect of yourself, or perhaps are feeling that a situation has become too out-there to handle. (*See Storms and Weather, right.*)

SKATING

"Skating on thin ice" is a common metaphor for a risky activity, but, in dreams, thick ice is almost as hazardous: A lake that is frozen solid could be telling us that we are failing to break through to the unconscious level below the surface, that we are not yet close to knowing ourselves. Skating skillfully and happily in a dream could indicate you are making good progress in some endeavor.

STORMS AND WEATHER

▲ A storm can be a metaphor for some catastrophic event out of your control.

For most of human history, we have been at the mercy of the elements, and the human mind has invented all manner of deities and mythical characters to account for phenomena such as raging storms, thunder and lightning, drought and heat. The idea that we can manipulate or appease the weather, that it is connected to our actions, still haunts both the waking and the dreaming mind. In a movie, we understand when a sorrowful character walks the streets through pouring rain: The weather is mirroring his mood. Our dreams use the same visual logic: Wind and rain tell us something about what we are feeling.

POSITIVE INTERPRETATION

Bright days and blue horizons are a metaphor for a carefree mood and a sense of happiness. Rain can be positive, suggesting regeneration and replenishment, and a rainbow suggests you have weathered the worst and things are looking brighter. (*See Sun and Sky, page 106.*)

NEGATIVE INTERPRETATION

Bad weather, unlike good weather, is an event in its own right. Both our conscious and our unconscious minds see extreme weather events—floods and blizzards—as departures from the norm. Storms, hurricanes, and tornadoes all suggest upheaval, emotional or physical. Droughts could indicate some kind of emotional deprivation in your life.

SNOW

Snow covers the landscape, hiding its features and contours, and can sometimes stand for concealment in dreams. Cold weather can also hint at a cold emotional climate (*see Ice, left*). Consider any words spoken in your winter dream and their pun potential: Could they reveal a deeper meaning?

THUNDER AND LIGHTNING

Light travels faster than sound, so lightning always comes before thunder. For this reason it is often an image of forewarning. Lightning can also indicate a brilliant idea, or a flash of inspiration. But often it denotes shock and a feeling of catastrophe, while thunder is the rumbling threat in the distance.

AN EARTHQUAKE

The ground shaking is a clear metaphor for insecurity, or some event (inner or outer) that is shaking up the foundations of your life. Escaping from the earthquake indicates confidence that you will overcome your difficulties.

WATER

▲ Hokusai's "The Waterfall" is a lovely evocation of release and letting go.

Water is essential for life, in reality as in dreams. A large body of water—a lake or an ocean—often represents the mind itself: The invisible unconscious that is below the surface, the conscious mind that we are aware of above it. Sometimes our dreams show us a boat or other vessel, the ship of the self, making its way across the water's surface, which is the boundary between the conscious and the unconscious.

POSITIVE INTERPRETATION

Still waters naturally indicate calm, but bear in mind that "still waters run deep": There could be things going on beneath the surface. Very often in dreams, we dive into the waters of the unconscious. Dreams of literal diving are a sign that you are getting in touch with hidden parts of yourself. What does your dream show you down there? Treasure and beautiful corals, and nothing to worry about? If there are wrecks and sea monsters, is there anything to help you face them?

NEGATIVE INTERPRETATION

Waters that are stormy or muddy indicate a turbulent mental state or outward situation. Consider your position within the dream: Are you tossed about by the waves or battling the gale at the wheel of your ship? If you are the captain of the ship, then perhaps your dream is showing you ways to deal with a tumultuous set of circumstances.

SEAS AND OCEANS

Dreams of oceans can represent the unknown and the fear of the unknown: It is all too easy to get lost at sea, because there is nothing to guide you. (*See Boats, page 81.*)

WATERFALLS

Waterfalls can stand for a gushing-out of emotion. But often they fall into a still pool of water—and in this way they can represent the uncontrolled release that leads to a state of greater calm.

CROSSING A RIVER OR STREAM

Dreaming of crossing a river is a clear image of an attempt, or need, to move on to a new phase or situation. The means of conveyance, especially if it is unusual, might indicate that you need to be inventive about how you make this next move. (*See Travel, page 74–83.*)

FIRE

▲ Fire is life, as well as destruction. We gaze into the flames for insight.

Awe and fear of fire are deeply rooted in the human psyche. The discovery of fire transformed the lives of early humans, and even today we can all be mesmerized by a flickering campfire or the dancing flames in a hearth. Most mythologies have tales about how fire is something divine that was given to humankind, and those tales usually involve theft, trickery, or retribution. Such stories hint at our conflicted relationship with fire: It provides warmth and light and is essential to our nourishment, but it is also destructive, painful, and dangerous. Fire symbols in dreams reflect all this ambiguity.

POSITIVE INTERPRETATION

A fire burning happily in a grate is usually a positive sign: It represents your own emotional warmth, as a house is nearly always a dream picture of the self, the rooms and their occupants standing for levels and corners of your own personality. If, in the dream, you are enjoying the fire, that indicates contentment with your emotional life.

NEGATIVE INTERPRETATION

A fire that is out of control—a forest fire, for example—is indicative of some unchecked emotion: anger, or perhaps a raging passion that is spiraling toward danger. A fire in the house is a clear warning from the unconscious mind to quench some inward emotional inferno.

A BURNING MATCH

A match is fire in miniature, representing a flicker or spark of insight that could ignite something much bigger. Extinguishing or blowing out a match is a sign that a possibility is no more.

LIGHTING A FIRE

Fires are hard to get going, but once started they grow bigger on their own. Is there some life aim that you are trying to undertake, without knowing exactly where it will lead you.

EXTINGUISHING A FIRE

The ability to quench a fire in a dream is a symbol of the control that you have, or would like to have, over a potentially damaging situation. It is surprising how often dreamers put out fires by urinating on them. This is a sign of self-reliance, that your ability to control affairs comes entirely from within yourself.

Animals

HORSES

▲ Horses carry us to our destination, and symbolize a drive toward progress.

Horses are symbols of strength and speed, and the stallion—male horse—is a common token of virility. The fact that these animals have long been used as a swift mode of transport means that, in a dream context, they can symbolize rapid progress toward a goal. Wild horses require taming before they can be useful to us, which makes the horse a good symbol of the process of exerting control over our own psyches. This is one of the many roles that horses can play in our dreams.

POSITIVE INTERPRETATION

Dreams of riding a horse indicate that you are making dynamic use of all the forces at your disposal. Horses can represent energy and power, and also sexual power, with horse and rider becoming one.

NEGATIVE INTERPRETATION

There may be dangerous aspects to any dream of horses. Are you clinging for life to a runaway horse? Have you been thrown from the horse? Are you being chased? How do you feel while these events occur? They all could indicate some threat to your safety in waking life, or a desire to get off the merry-go-round on which you find yourself.

EQUINE EVENTS

If you dream of horse-racing, did you win? The type of event matters: Show-jumping is about overcoming obstacles; dressage about absolute mastery; and hunting about some unacknowledged inner pursuit.

DONKEYS

Donkeys (or asses) are beasts of burden and can stand for emotional baggage. They are also symbols of stupidity and stubbornness—might this be what they represent in your dreams?

MULES

An infertile cross between a horse and a donkey, in a dream a mule could stand for a partnership (or a dual aspect of yourself) that has no future. Like the donkey, mules are known for carrying goods and therefore could point to some emotional weight that you are carrying.

◀ Animals have some abilities far superior to our own; in dreams they represent the characteristics they embody—ones that we covet or fear.

ANIMALS

COWS, SHEEP, AND GOATS

▲ The peaceful cow is a mother, but one that we subvert for our own purposes.

Cows are mother figures—symbols of nurture, fertility, and generosity. A dream of a cow is almost certain to have some connection to the maternal. Sheep can represent community, the undifferentiated group, while goats in many cultures stand for lust and virility. In dreams the symbolism of goats can take a more subtle form: Libido (as Freud understood it) means the creative urge rather than mere sexual desire.

POSITIVE INTERPRETATION

Dreams of cows can represent the sacred—as they do in Hinduism. A dream of goats can sometimes stand for the urge to get ahead in life, to climb life's slopes with the nimble grace of a mountain goat. Sheep can be an picture of acceptance; the mirror image of their passivity.

NEGATIVE INTERPRETATION

As cows represent the feminine, so bulls stand for the masculine. A dream of a bullfight or perhaps a "bull in a china shop," might indicate a need to rein in the thrusting, aggressive part of the psyche. Goats, because they will eat almost anything, can represent a lack of discrimination. Sheep may imply you are unthinkingly following the majority.

LAMBS

Lambs are often portrayed as the epitome of helplessness or the innocence of childhood. Because of their sacrificial role in the Bible's Old Testament stories, they can also imply selflessness or self-denial.

RAMS

A ram can represent two almost opposite concepts. On the one hand, it stands for instinct and sexual drive, because rams are held to be sexually rampant. On the other, the curled horns on the head are like projections of the brain—so a butting ram can be an image of the intellect aggressively deployed to solve a problem.

MILKING A COW

The act of milking a cow can represent the idea of taking something that is not willingly given. It can also have a kind of dual sexual aspect, since udders are the exaggerated bovine equivalent of women's breasts and the milking process bears a resemblance to the act of ejaculation.

WOLVES
AND FOXES

▲ The Arctic fox can represent adaptability to one's environment.

Wolves are very ambivalent dream symbols. They are the voracious villains of many European folktales, but in Roman mythology they were associated with Apollo, the sun god, and so can be (like the sun) a token of the animus or male principle. In Native American traditions, wolves are benevolent guides and holders of knowledge. Foxes often stand for quick-wittedness and cunning.

POSITIVE INTERPRETATION

In the classical tradition, the twin infants Romulus and Remus, founders of Rome, were suckled by a she-wolf, and wolves in dreams sometimes imply help coming from an unexpected source—one that one might even expect to be hostile. Although foxes are often negative symbols, they can also represent creativity and sexual attractiveness.

NEGATIVE INTERPRETATION

Wolves hunt in packs and are fearsome killers. For this reason they are often adopted as a symbol by military organizations and in dreams they can stand for life-and-death conflict. Foxes usually represent a liar or cheat (or perhaps the deceptive aspect of yourself). Since they are held to kill for pleasure, they can be symbols of needless destruction.

WOLVES EATING

A dream of feeding wolves can be a graphic representation of a fierce spiritual hunger. But if the dream scene is distressing or disgusting, that might suggest that you are allowing the psyche to feed of the carcass of some dead or redundant situation. Perhaps you urgently need to let something go.

HOWLING AT THE MOON

The moon usually stands for the feminine principle. A dream of wolves howling at the moon can therefore imply that the psyche is desperate to access this side of itself, the part that engenders empathy, nurture, imagination, and spirituality.

A FOXHUNT

If you dream that you are the fox being hunted, this is a clear metaphor for some escape that you need to make in waking life. If you are one of the hunters, think about what the fox might represent: Do you crave the fox's craftiness?

ANIMALS

CATS

▲ Kittens can represent our playful side, or a sense of family.

Cats are protectors of the home, first domesticated to keep down mice and other vermin. In dreams, the house is often a symbol of the dreamer's own psyche, so the presence of a cat can represent the factors that promote the dreamer's sense of mental and emotional stability. A dream of a cat leaving the house can imply the opposite: That the dreamer's equilibrium is at risk. Cats often stand for the anima—the female aspect of the psyche—so your dream could also suggest that you need to access the feminine part of yourself.

POSITIVE INTERPRETATION

The enviable self-assurance of the domestic cat makes it a symbol of wisdom and meditation. In cultures from Japan to Egypt cats have been variously seen as harbingers of good fortune, tokens of prosperity, and guarantors of good harvests and new life. All these positive aspects of cat lore can be encountered in dreams.

NEGATIVE INTERPRETATION

Cats are creatures of the night and can sometimes have a sinister meaning in dreams. In former times, they were seen as the familiars of witches and in some cultures black cats are omens of bad luck. They are also associated with heresy, and in a dream context can stand for wrong-headed ideas. "Cattiness" is petty spite and this could be another dream meaning.

A CAT WITH PREY

Cats play with their prey, and this dream could signify a fear that someone is playing with you. If you dream that a cat brings you an object, then consider what that gift might represent.

A CAT IN A TREE

Cats stuck in trees are a stock situation in films and comedies. Usually, the moment someone attempts a rescue, the cat blithely skips down to the ground on its own. A dream of a cat in a tree might be an indication that you can rectify a seemingly insoluble issue yourself—if only you have a mind to.

NINE LIVES

Any reference to a cat's nine live in a dream indicates your inner resourcefulness and ability to recover from difficulty or overcome multiple or multifaceted problems.

CAT'S EYES

Since cats are known for their good night vision, a dream in which cat's eyes are significant can suggest you are seeing the light in a dark or difficult situation.

DOGS

▲ The St. Bernard, here by de Gempt, is the rescuer of lost and injured travelers.

Dogs are humanity's oldest animal companions; they were domesticated more than 15,000 years ago. In dreams, they stand for those parts of our nature that we have brought completely under our own control. They can also represent our ability to change the external world, as the vast variety of dog breeds is entirely attributable to human activity. Dogs in all their diversity are, like thoughts, living inventions of the human mind.

POSITIVE INTERPRETATION

You may well dream of a particular dog, perhaps a beloved pet. If so, do as you would with the human inhabitants of your dream world—ask yourself what the dog represents to you. You may well turn to positive attributes such as loyalty, devotion, and unconditional love. A barking dog could be reassurance that someone's bark is worse than their bite. Dogs represent protection, so may reflect feelings that you are defending yourself or that someone else is looking out for you.

NEGATIVE INTERPRETATION

Dogs hunt in packs, so a dream about dogs can reference feelings of being at the mercy of a certain group, or being hunted down in some way. Dogs can be expelled from the home and sent to sleep outside (in the doghouse), so they can represent exclusion and punishment.

A DOG BITE

Dreaming that you are bitten by a dog signifies feeling under attack, perhaps by someone who is defending what they see as their territory. Since dogs are known for their loyalty, this can also mean that someone you considered a friend or ally has betrayed you.

A GUIDE DOG

If you dream of a guide dog, it may well be that you feel you need outside help to achieve some vital insight. If you dream that you are yourself the dog, the unconscious mind may be telling you that your own intuition is more far-reaching than you realize.

SPECIFIC BREEDS

The human qualities that we ascribe to different breeds can serve as signals in our dreams: Poodles are seen as subservient, Alsatians as vigilant, terriers as persistent, and rottweilers as violent. What might these breeds and their qualities betoken in your life?

ANIMALS

RABBITS AND HARES

▲ The rabbits of *Watership Down* symbolize the synergy of group action.

In some African folktales, the hare was seen as a clever trickster. When these stories were retold in America by generations of slaves, the hare became the now famous Br'er Rabbit. The idea that rabbits are resourceful and brave was revisited and reinforced in Richard Adams' novel *Watership Down*. Dreams of rabbits, depending on their context, might well be a call to show rabbit-like endeavor and courage.

POSITIVE INTERPRETATION

Hares are often associated with the moon (in China and Japan, it is believed that the dark patches on the moon's surface resemble a hare). This means that a dream hare can be a symbol of the female, like the moon itself. They also represent intuition and creative ideas, as well as fast progress. Known for their fast breeding habits, rabbits represent sexual urges and fertility, abundance, and also community. They are a symbol of good fortune.

NEGATIVE INTERPRETATION

Because they increase their population so quickly, rabbits in dreams can be metaphors for situations that are mushrooming out of control, especially if, in the dream, the animals are present in overwhelming numbers. Hares can stand for complacency—as in the fable of the tortoise and the hare.

RABBITS AND SEX

Both rabbits and hares have long been seen as symbols of lust and promiscuity. This association goes back to the Greeks, who regarded the hare as the animal of Aphrodite, the goddess of love.

RABBIT HOLES

It follows that dreams of rabbit holes in a mound, or of rabbits disappearing into holes, can be metaphors for sex and the female genitalia. Rabbit holes or subterranean warrens can more viscerally imply a desire to escape back to the womb, which is a place of safety.

EARS OF THE RABBIT AND HARE

Sharp hearing gives rabbits and hares a seemingly uncanny ability to sense danger. If rabbit ears are significant in your dream, this could be a warning to be on the lookout.

MICE AND RATS

▲ A mouse can symbolize a minor problem that is gnawing away at you.

The poet Robert Burns wrote about "the best-laid schemes of mice an' men." This is a reference to the fact that humans can be as powerless and at the mercy of fate as little mice. In dreams, mice can be stand-ins for ourselves, like tiny actors on the dreamworld stage, and symbols of vulnerability. The same is rarely true of rats, which we see as invasive enemies of our own kind.

POSITIVE INTERPRETATION

Although mice are vulnerable, they can have an impact that is out of proportion to their size: Think of the attractive (but false) idea that elephants are terrified of mice. We need to believe—in our waking lives and in our dreams—that the insignificant sometimes triumph over the powerful, and a mouse may be the unconscious mind's vehicle for showing this.

NEGATIVE INTERPRETATION

Swarms of mice and rats both can be visual ciphers for the spread of disease and for infestation. In a dream the epidemic that they represent might be metaphorical: An unhealthy idea that infects a community or the individual consciousness.

RATS AND SEWERS

We feel disgust for the rodents that live beneath us, in the dirtiest part of the urban infrastructure. Dream rats emerging from the sewers might represent unpleasant thoughts and desires that we are unwilling to face and would rather keep hidden down below, out of sight of the conscious mind.

A MOUSETRAP

The thing about a mousetrap is: If you know one is there, you can easily avoid it. Could this dream be telling you to remain on the alert?

RATLIKE QUALITIES

In Chinese culture the rat symbolizes hard work and prosperity, and the Romans believed that they were good luck—but otherwise this rodent's associations are almost entirely negative. Rats can stand for betrayal, irritability, and narrow self-interest (as in rats leaving a sinking ship).

ANIMALS

BIRDS

Birds constitute a rich area of dream lore because they are such a varied class of animal: In a dream, a kestrel or an owl will mean something different from a sparrow or a wren. Sometimes it will be up to you to delve into your own mind for the meaning of a particular bird. We humans have long observed or exploited many avian species, and we are sometimes envious of their capabilities—above all their effortless gift of flight. For these reasons, birds haunt our imaginations and our dreams.

POSITIVE INTERPRETATION

Birds generally stand for freedom or the longing for freedom—we have all had the experience of watching a bird soar away and wishing we could do the same. Birds also represent the female principle: It is no coincidence that the word "chick" is a slang term for a woman in American English, or that the word "bird" has much the same connotations in British slang.

NEGATIVE INTERPRETATION

Birds can be a sinister presence—a fact exploited brilliantly by Alfred Hitchcock in his 1963 horror movie *The Birds*. Certain species have morbid associations: Crows and ravens, with their black plumage, are harbingers of death; we see the natural behavior of magpies as thievery, and we use the word "vulture" for people who exploit the misfortunes of others. All these waking ideas can be present in our dreams.

SWANS

Swans resemble beautiful curving question marks moving across a lake or river—and can stand for the inquiring conscious mind, patrolling the border with the unconscious, which is represented by the surface of the water.

PARROTS

Caged birds are symbols of restriction, entrapment, and the desire to escape. Parrots are a special case because—in dreams as in life—they can speak to us. In this way they represent a need to articulate. That might be the only way to get the door open and fly free.

DOVES AND CUCKOOS

These are two birds with strong mythic associations. Doves are symbols of love and togetherness, and of the coming of peace at the end of a time of conflict. Cuckoos are rather sinister to us, because of their practice of laying their eggs in other birds' nest. They stand for deception and usurpation.

FLIGHTLESS BIRDS

All flightless birds—emus, ostriches, penguins—were once creatures of the air. They gave up flying in order to flourish in a different evolutionary niche. In dreams, these birds often stand for the sacrifices we make to get on.

BIRDS OF PREY

Birds of prey are ambivalent symbols. On the one hand they are beautiful and magnificent in flight; it is no coincidence that they often feature on flags and other national symbols as the embodiment of proud authority. They can represent farsightedness and wisdom (like the owl). But they are also pitiless—ruthless killers of weaker, slower animals.

BIRD NAMES

The names of bird species can open the way to unconscious wordplay. Consider the puns, metaphors, or homophones that could be hidden within the name of the bird that you have dreamt of. It may seem far-fetched that such wordplay could signify deeper meaning in dreams, but these are exactly the allusive ways in which the unconscious presents repressed or difficult ideas to us.

▲ This colored etching from circa 1820 shows a woodpecker, bullfinch, and other birds perched on or near a tree. Birds can represent flight and freedom in a dream.

SNAKES AND OTHER REPTILES

▲ Snakes often go unseen and can be a metaphor for a sense of hidden danger.

The snake is the most common reptile to make an appearance in dreams. It can symbolize a range of things. It is, on a Freudian level, one of many phallic symbols. But it also has various mythic associations that our dreams can access. In Greek mythology, serpents are often an enemy of humankind. Think of the many-headed hydra that grows two heads when one is chopped off: We all have hydra-like problems in our lives—situations that just get worse when we try to address them.

POSITIVE INTERPRETATION

A snake entwined around a long-stemmed cup is a symbol known as the bowl of Hygieia, while a snake or two climbing a stick is called the rod of Asclepius: Both represent healing. And snakes, because they periodically shed their skins, are often dream symbols of fresh starts and new beginnings.

NEGATIVE INTERPRETATION

In the biblical story of Adam and Eve, the snake is the embodiment of a potentially disastrous temptation. Some lizards have the alarming ability to shed their tail when threatened: Is there some painful sacrifice that you need to make so as to survive or move forward?

DINOSAURS

However terrifying dinosaurs may appear in our dreams or in movies such as *Jurassic Park*, they were gone long before humans ever walked on Earth. If you dream of dinosaurs, the danger that they represent is not real. They also represent outdated ideas.

ALLIGATORS AND CROCODILES

Appearing like harmless floating logs in the water, alligators and crocodiles can suddenly reveal themselves to be a deadly danger. If you dream of a crocodile, your unconscious might be warning you that you are facing a greater hazard than you realize.

A SERPENT SWALLOWING ITS TAIL

This is an image that crops up in diverse cultures and many different ages. Known as the Ouroboros, it is a positive symbol of eternity, wholeness, and rebirth.

INSECTS
AND SPIDERS

▲ Butterflies are industrious and creative, and remind us that life is short.

We think that we despise insects, and certainly humanity has an ancient and instinctive fear of the ones that can poison us or spread disease. But in our dreams, we tap into a deeper strain of understanding: On a mythic level we see spiders that persevere, as well as ants that work for the common good, and bees giving devoted service to their queen. In dreams, insects have human attributes that we can admire and draw lessons from.

POSITIVE INTERPRETATION

Many insects have positive dream symbolism because they benefit mankind. Bees stand for generosity, because they are an essential part of the food-growing process and because they freely share their honey. Butterflies are symbols of fragility, but also of the transformational power of passing time—of the potential for beauty to emerge from any situation.

NEGATIVE INTERPRETATION

Flies are symbols of decay and putrefaction, and in dreams they can represent anything that is spoiled beyond redemption. There is a touch of evil about them. Beelzebub, which is one name for the devil, means "Lord of the Flies." Scorpions are another creature with negative associations: Their sinister arching sting is dangerous, out of all proportion to the size of the animal—and it strikes, treacherously, from behind.

SPIDERS

The spider can symbolize creativity as it spins a complex web, which could be a web of connections or the web of life. Once caught, its prey is powerless to escape, just as we may feel trapped in a web of deception.

BEETLES

Ladybugs are one of the gardener's helpmeets and can stand for the people or things that aid our growth. All beetles can be a lesson in how hard work can reap reward. The dung beetle is also known as the "scarab," and to the ancient Egyptians was a symbol of regeneration. This sense can easily crop up in dreams.

HUMANS BECOMING INSECTS

This idea occurs in movies (*The Fly*) and in literature (Franz Kafka's *Metamorphosis*). Was it empowering to fly almost invisibly? Did you feel vulnerable? Were you pleased, or disgusted? Your own sensations and emotions are the best clue to the meaning of the dream.

ANIMALS

DOLPHINS
AND WHALES

▲ A dream whale hunt may indicate that success is possible with teamwork.

Dolphins and whales are mammals—which is to say that they evolved from land-based animals. In some distant time, they returned to the sea. This makes them a potent symbol of adaptability, as well as of the circular nature of existence. We all come from some obscure and hidden oblivion, and we all return to it. Dreams of dolphins and whales are a reminder of this. They can also represent intelligence and communication skills—attributes they are known for.

POSITIVE INTERPRETATION

Dreams of these magnificent animals can offer insights into (or communication from) the deeper parts of the mind, represented by the ocean itself. Throughout history, dolphins have been seen as the helpers of humankind, so dream dolphins can be an indication of some aid that is available to you, particularly in an affair of the heart (Cupid, the god of sexual desire, is often depicted riding on a dolphin).

NEGATIVE INTERPRETATION

A beached whale is a symbol of total helplessness—made worse by the fact that the creature's natural strengths, its size and its oceangoing form, have been transformed by circumstance into fatal weakness. Does this chime with some situation in your waking life?

WATCHING WHALES AND DOLPHINS

If you dream of dolphins or whales breaking the surface of the ocean, it may be that your unconscious is aware of certain thoughts coming to the attention of the conscious mind. This is a dream indicating that you are making progress in your quest to better understand yourself.

WHALE HUNTING

If you are hunting a whale in your dream, that may be an indication that you are taking on something much bigger than yourself. However, if you form part of a hunting party, this could signify success is possible with teamwork. If you feel sadness in the dream, then the whale may represent spirituality—which you are denying.

SHARKS

Sharks are dangerous predators, and so they can symbolize someone who pursues his or her desires regardless of the consequences. However, more positively, sharks famously have to keep moving forward in order to survive: If you dream of a shark, it may be a message that you should persevere.

FISH AND SEA CREATURES

▲ Consider how many fish are present in a group; the number may be significant.

The sea is swarming with creatures of all shapes and varieties, just as the mind teems with thoughts of every stripe and emotions of every hue. Sea creatures can be representative of our own mental and temperamental process: Little fishes, secret wishes. Fish, for the most part, live in a world that is only partly accessible to us, or at least not our natural habitat. And so there is always an element of the unattainable about their presence in our dreams: They are something hard to grasp, or they slip out of reach.

POSITIVE INTERPRETATION

Dreams of sea creatures can be very uplifting, especially if you find that you can breathe underwater. A pleasant dream of swimming in a school of fish can suggest community and feeling accepted. Fishes can also represent fertility or abundance.

NEGATIVE INTERPRETATION

Some sea creatures can be threatening to us in our dreams. The human imagination is haunted by sea monsters—Scotland's Loch Ness monster Nessie, the *havhest* (sea horse) of Nordic myth, the sleeping *kraken*. They all look like fearsome images of the bestial parts of human nature, lurking in the depths of the mind. Something "fishy" is questionable, while feeling like "a fish out of water" suggests being out of place.

FISHING

To fish is to search. If you dream of fishing in the ocean, of trawling deep waters from a ship, or of diving down to spear your quarry, then you are probably looking at a graphic picture of your emotional and spiritual journey. In your dream, was your fishing trip a success?

DEAD FISH

This is a dream about disappointment or failure. Since fish are associated with unconscious desires, it could mean the death of an idea or an unacknowledged wish.

NAMES FOR SEA CREATURES

The designations of fish provide another opportunity for the unconscious mind to indulge its love of wordplay. As with other animals, consider the name of any specific species in your dreams and what this could point to other than its literal interpretation.

LIONS AND BIG CATS

▲ The majestic tiger represents ferocity and danger, and sexual power.

We like to think of lions, and other species belonging to the subfamily *Panthera*, as "big cats." It amuses and intrigues us to see them as overgrown versions of the harmless domestic cat. Why? Because our collective unconscious recognizes that there are things within ourselves—painful experiences, disappointments, troubling memories—that can grow wild and become dangerous to us. The "big cat" idea reflects a truth about human nature, and it can make its way into our dreams.

POSITIVE INTERPRETATION

Lions have associations of kingship and courage. If you see yourself in a dream as a lion, that speaks to your sense of your own authority and strength. A lioness is famous for ferociously protecting her young: Is there a project—your baby—that you are fighting for?

NEGATIVE INTERPRETATION

The lion, as the archetypal wild beast, represents the threat that the untamed id presents to the moral part of your personality. In a dream, this could suggest that base instincts continue, on occasion, to triumph over higher spiritual aspirations. Fearing a lion could also signify anxiety about an authority figure in your life.

FACING LIONS

It is telling if you find yourself in the presence of lions that do not harm you. This image crops up in the biblical story of the prophet Daniel, among other places, and implies that you have the ability to emerge unscathed from a coming ordeal.

CHEETAHS AND LEOPARDS

The leopard, proverbially, cannot change its spots—it is a slave to its nature. Is this is an association that resonates with you? Both the leopard and cheetah are images of camouflage, and perhaps indicate duplicity.

TIGERS

In the folklore of the East, tigers are symbols of anger and war. That sense is present in the expression "to grasp a tiger by the tail," meaning to risk harm through inadequate precautions against an aggressor. Tigers are often depicted as man-eaters and can represent emotions eating away at your soul. These powerful animals can also indicate sexual power.

ELEPHANTS AND LARGE ANIMALS

▲ In a dream, the elephant indicates you are dealing with something big.

To the human mind, elephants and their ancestors are the personification of bigness; we speak of any enormous thing as being "mammoth." In Hindu mythology, the world rests on the back of four elephants—and in dreams, too, they can represent stability and strength. Since they are said never to forget, elephants can also symbolize memory.

POSITIVE INTERPRETATION

Elephants are on the whole gentle creatures, or seem so to us. In our dreams they can be a symbol of forbearance, steadfastness, and faithfulness. They are proverbially thick-skinned, untroubled by the buzzing flies and the tiny fleabites. So a dream elephant could be a messenger telling us not to "sweat the small stuff."

NEGATIVE INTERPRETATION

We have all heard the expression "the elephant in the room," meaning our desire to skirt difficult but obvious problems. It is part of the function of our dreams to make us acknowledge the elephants that intrusively crowd the mansion of the mind. Elephants and other large animals could also represent negative feelings about being overweight or heavy.

HIPPOS AND RHINOS

The hippopotamus is (erroneously) perceived as a gentle animal, partly because it is protective toward its young. The ancient Egyptian divinity Taweret, depicted as part-hippo, was the goddess of pregnancy and childbirth. These associations can seep down into our dreams. Rhinoceroses can represent the male principle—partly because their horns have a phallic appearance.

BEARS

The apparently cuddly bear is also a ferocious fighter, so consider these dual aspects of its character. Perhaps your dream bear is a reference to a childhood toy?

GIRAFFES

Giraffes, because of their enormous reach, often stand for ambition in dreams. They can also signal cooperation in pursuit of a goal, because they were long believed to be a hybrid of two animals, the camel and the leopard.

MYTHICAL BEASTS AND BEINGS

It is a core fact of dream interpretation that our night visions draw on the same deep well of imagery and narrative as myths and legends. They are all part of the same symbolic data bank that Jung called the "collective unconscious." Strange animals and otherworldly races are part of the cast of characters in the collective unconscious, and many of them are hybrids—half human, half animal, or a blend of two animals. Our minds seem to feel a need to create these creatures and to give them meaning.

POSITIVE INTERPRETATION

Many mythological beasts are helpers to humanity. The centaur, or man-horse, is a symbol both of deep wisdom and of healing. Unicorns are white horses (or sometimes deer) with a single horn: They often stand for something elusive, a truth that is just beyond our grasp. The silent and inscrutable sphinx (part-human, part-lion) stands for all the things that we cannot know—which, after all, is most things.

NEGATIVE INTERPRETATION

Many of the creatures of the imagination are malevolent. The werewolf is the violent animal within each of us. Vampires are creatures that steal our blood and with it our life force; is someone sucking the life from you or a project?

DRAGONS

Dragons are snakes writ large, and so in dreams can be a picture of the libido, the strong force that is sometimes phallic, often creative, occasionally destructive. Dreams of defeating a dragon—like Bilbo Baggins in *The Hobbit* or St. George in Christian myth—are concerned with one's own struggle with inner monsters.

MERPEOPLE

Mermaids and mermen—part human, part fish—are ambivalent symbols. Sometimes they are benevolent; other times they seem bent on drawing human victims to disaster. As sea creatures, but rational beings too, they can stand for the attempt to infiltrate human reason into the murky depths of the unconscious mind.

GRIFFINS

A griffin is a mythical beast with the head and wings of an eagle and the body of a lion. In dreams, it can represent the search for higher things (the soaring eagle) and the struggle against the distractions of human existence (the earthbound, appetite-driven lion).

FAUNS

Fauns are part human, part goat. They are often sexual symbols, since in classical myth they are associated with unfettered passion (and are often depicted with enormous phalluses). On a more gentle and genteel level, they represent unalloyed joy, the simple pleasures of community and human interaction.

PHOENIXES

A phoenix is a firebird that is consumed in flames and then reborn from its own ashes. It is a symbol of the rebirth that we see everywhere in nature and in human affairs: When one thing ends, it gives rise to a new beginning or to a

fresh opportunity. If you dream of a phoenix, you are tapping into this universal truth and perhaps drawing strength from it.

GIANTS AND FAIRIES

Jung pointed out that, as small children, we all inhabit a world of giants: They are the adults who surround us. So dreams of giants often point us toward something that happened in childhood, when everyone we knew and loved was several times taller than our own self.

▲ The dragon slayer—a symbol of struggle and power—is found in myths drawn from across the world. This image is from 17th-century India.

ANIMALS

ANIMAL-RELATED OBJECTS

Our daily lives are filled with objects that come from animals, though perhaps less so than in past times. Feathers and fur, shells and bones, pelts and fleeces—all of these things can become the meaningful bric-a-brac of our dreams lives. The fact that we use these things in a host of different ways means that the precise symbolism can vary greatly, and much will depend on subjective associations. But nevertheless, there are universal symbols connected with animal-related objects.

POSITIVE INTERPRETATION

Many animal-related objects can be positively interpreted. A bird's nest or a burrow might symbolize a secure place that you have carved out for yourself; if you follow animal tracks, that indicates that you know the path you should be taking (the type of animal you are tracking may well be significant); a hive or a termite mound can stand for fruitful cooperation.

NEGATIVE INTERPRETATION

There are countless ways in which animal-related objects can have a negative aspect. Take spiders' webs: They are, after all, killing zones, traps laid by dangerous predators. What is your attitude to the spiders' web in your dream? White feathers have traditionally been used as a badge of cowardice: Is your unconscious reproaching you with something that you have not found the courage to face?

BONES

Animal bones were humanity's earliest tools, and to dream of bones is to see yourself seeking out the most fundamental and basic solution to a problem—especially if you are wielding the bone in some way. A wishbone is not usually about desires, but about choices: The Y-shaped bone represents two possible paths that you might take.

FLEECE

The fleece of a sheep is a source of warmth and comfort—and one that does not cost the giver dearly. In your dream, are you wearing a fleece or is someone else wearing yours? The act of shearing a sheep represents the idea of revealing what is hidden beneath in a way that is cathartic and gives relief.

FUR

If you dream of wearing fur, consider your associations with the animal that the pelt comes from. It is likely that your unconscious is telling you to take on the attributes of that animal, as you perceive them: To be commanding like a lion, sly as a fox, or solitary as a tiger.

SHELLS

Some shells, because of their shape and convolutions, serve as yonic symbols—that is, disguised visual references to the female genitalia. They often serve this purpose in dreams. Shells can also signify legacy as they are what remains when the sea creature that grew in the shell has died.

FEATHERS

The dream symbolism of feathers is very rich. For centuries, feather quills were used for writing—and so can signify articulacy and the need to speak out. Downy feathers are used for pillows and mattresses, and can point to the warmth and security of the womb. A feather

borne aloft in the air might be a picture of a
personal insight floating to the surface of the
conscious mind.

HORNS

Animal horns are a clear phallic symbol, both
visually and because "horn" is a slang term for
an erection. But a horn is also a sounded
warning, an alarm. Bear this sense in mind,
along with any associations that you might have
with the animal from which the horn derives.

▲ When feathers are used with
extravagance and for adornment, your
dream could be pointing to some form
of vanity or showmanship.

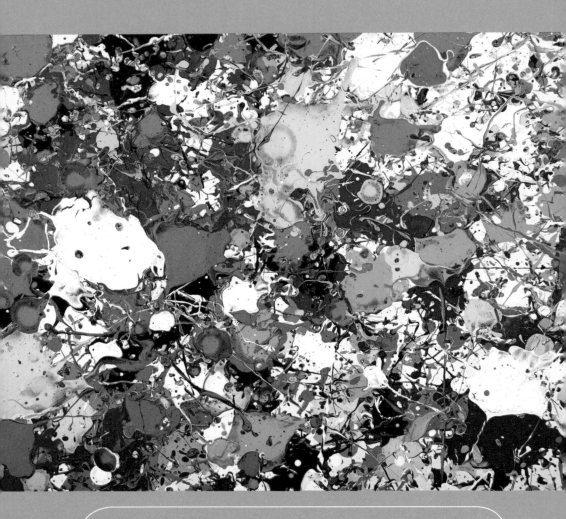

Colors

RED

▲ Red blooms denote love, but poppies also signify war and remembrance.

Red is a very physical color. Of all the colors of the spectrum, this is the one that has the strongest impact on us: Looking at a swatch of red can increase the heartbeat and breathing rate. It is, of course, the color of blood—the life energy that flows through us—and the color of blushing, which is the physiological signal of heightened emotion. For this reason, dreams in which red predominates are often connected to feelings of arousal, anger, heat, or energy in its wider context.

POSITIVE INTERPRETATIONS

The main association with red is passion and potency, so a dream in which red is significant may be about desire or the passion you are putting into an area of your life. Think about what is red in your dream, as this could signal where you should be putting your energies.

NEGATIVE INTERPRETATIONS

Red gives the subliminal message of danger. Are you involved in something risky or is your unconscious mind trying to tell you to "stop"? As the color of dominance, it may also be warning you about someone or something. Is there a power struggle playing out in your waking life, or are you very angry with someone? Red is the color of blood and therefore can symbolize pain and injury. (*See Blood, page 44.*)

RED FLOWERS

These are the archetypal symbol of romantic love, especially red roses. Are the flowers being given, and who are the giver and receiver? If the flowers are wilting or discarded, this suggests a romantic relationship is under threat.

RED CARPET

A symbol of wealth and praise, red carpets are laid out for high-status individuals at events. Dreaming of a red carpet can signify that you have confidence in your worth or life path, or perhaps are seeking public affirmation for your achievements.

OTHER MEANINGS OF RED

A red flag can signify provocation, as in the red cape of the matador. Things that are unnaturally red—a red sea or a blood-red sky—signify feelings of unease in the dreamer, perhaps a fear of some ominous turn of events.

◀ If a color is significant in your dream, consider your personal associations with it as well as cultural references.

PINK

▲ Pink often relates to childhood, as in George Romney's painting.

The softer side of red, pink has some of the same connotations albeit in a gentler form. It is associated with love, but rather than the fiery passions of red, pink represents a seduction and affection. It can also represent kindness, compassion, and unconditional love. In waking life, pink is known to have a relaxing or pacifying effect—in one famous experiment, the walls and ceiling of prison cells were painted this color and a reduction in prisoners' aggression was noted. Is there someone in the dream who needs pacifying or neutralizing?

POSITIVE INTERPRETATION

Pink has many positive associations, including good health and happiness. It is linked with femininity and traditionally feminine virtues such as compassion and charm. In a dream, it may represent a desire to connect with these qualities or with the feminine side of yourself (this goes for men as well as women). Pink is a youthful color, often linked with innocence and childhood.

NEGATIVE INTERPRETATION

If pale pink is significant in your dream, that may reflect a desire to give up the burdens of adulthood and be looked after; dreaming of a room with pink walls could be a referencing the total dependence of being in the womb.

PINK FLOWERS

Pink flowers are traditionally given to represent affection and friendship as well as gratitude. If you receive a pink bouquet in a dream this can be a sign that you feel appreciated.

PINK FOODS

These are the foods most commonly associated with sweetness. Cotton candy or pink sweets could represent childhood pleasures and a longing to enjoy them once more. If the food is not usually this color, then the dream may be suggesting artificiality—is someone in your waking life less sweet than they appear?

PINK CLOTHES

Dressing or covering yourself in pink may be a way of signaling a need for love and attention, or it could be a proud acceptance of sexuality or of femininity, depending on the dreamer.

ORANGE

▲ Turner made brilliant use of exuberant orange in this dreamlike composition.

This brilliant hue is the color of the tropical sun and has associations of optimism, positivity, and vitality. It's often a color chosen to represent political movements because it carries with it a feeling of newness and hope. If orange predominates in a dream it often reflects some sort of positive change, or perhaps it reveals to the dreamer where his or her energies may best be directed. Since the color is so vivacious and eye-catching, it may also demonstrate a wish to be noticed.

POSITIVE INTERPRETATION

Orange is a color of balance and warmth, combining the primal physicality of red with the mental focus of yellow. Dreams of orange things therefore suggest that some kind of equilibrium has been reached. Orange is also a color linked with frivolity and fun. Is your unconscious encouraging you to lighten up in some way?

NEGATIVE INTERPRETATION

Orange, along with yellow, is the color chosen for high-visibility clothing and safety equipment, such as rafts and the misnamed "black box" of an airplane. A dream of orange could be about risk or danger—is the dream calling your attention to some peril?

FALL HUES

Rustic orange, saffron, and dull reds are the colors of fall, a time when things die down before a time of essential rest. Dreams about the fall season can illustrate the end of one stage of life, and signal that it is time to reflect and prepare for a new one.

ORANGE ROBES

Buddhist monks often wear robes of orange, the color of enlightenment. Orange is a sacred color in Hinduism, too. If you are wearing orange robes in your dream this could betoken some kind of spiritual yearning.

ORANGES

The sweet fruits are renowned for their nutrients and juiciness, so this can be a dream symbol of vitality. If the orange is sour or flavorless, that suggests an unexpected lack of energy in your waking life. The segments of an orange may be significant: Is there some division, some lack of wholeness, that is occupying your unconscious mind?

YELLOW

▲ Artists understand the language of color. Yellow signifies happiness.

Yellow is the color of sunshine and is also held to be the color of the mind, symbolizing the intellect and clarity of thought. It is closely related to gold and can stand for prosperity. Many people dislike yellow: Your personal feelings about this color, or any other color come to that, may be as significant in your dream as any cultural associations.

POSITIVE INTERPRETATION

Yellow can suggest that you are turning your face toward the light or being guided by a light, so might point to some kind of religious or spiritual awakening. It can also suggest radiance in other contexts—good health or positive (sunny) feelings toward another person. Soft yellows symbolize innocence and childhood.

NEGATIVE INTERPRETATION

Yellow is the color most strongly associated with cowardice and treachery and this negative reference might crop up in a dream. Are you—or is someone else—being cowardly and refusing to stick up for your beliefs? Yellow can also suggest sickness, especially if the hue is itself a bilious one.

SPRING FLOWERS

The first flowers to emerge in spring are often yellow and as such carry a message of renewal and hope. If you are giving yellow flowers to someone, or being given them in a dream, this suggests a need to revitalize your connection with that individual.

GOLD

This hue in a dream has an obvious connection with wealth (gold coins and jewelry), and can infer feelings of emotional as well as material value. If something unusual is gold in your dream this could be a suggestion that you should give greater value or pay greater heed to that object or person in real life.

WARNING SIGNS

Yellow is the most visible of colors to the human eye and for this reason is often used for hazard signs; it also signals caution in the natural world especially when combined with black (as in wasps). Is your dream self being warned to look out for some hidden danger?

GREEN

▲ Rossetti's "The Day Dream" draws on the association of green with relaxation.

Green, the color of a fertile landscape, is known to be the most relaxing hue to the human eye. It represents growth and abundance—and this has led to a more stylized meaning for green—wealth and money. It's not surprising that so many countries have green banknotes. But at the deepest level, green is the signal that a place is habitable and can provide for life.

POSITIVE INTERPRETATIONS

Green can signal that you feel all is flourishing in your world; that you are in, or about to enter, a new period of growth and development; or that you are looking for something fresh and new. Sometimes the appearance of green in a dream indicates a need for healing and escape, to find tranquility and peace away from it all.

NEGATIVE INTERPRETATION

A very dark or sickly green is a color linked to envy and jealousy. Green water is often stagnant; since water is connected to the emotions, this could suggest that you are stagnating in a relationship or emotional issue. Many things go green when rotten—could this be the meaning implied in your dream? Conversely, certain fruits are green when underripe: Who or what is not ready?

GREEN LIGHTS

Green has been chosen as the "go" signal for traffic lights because we have a primal sense that green is positive and healthy. It is also often the color used for "on" buttons, with red being the "off." For this reason, a "green light" in a dream may be suggesting that some undertaking in waking life can go ahead.

GREEN ROOMS

TV studios traditionally painted their guests' waiting area green, so dreaming of a green room could be a subliminal reference to this. Are you readying yourself to show your talents or achievements to the world at large?

GREEN GEMS OR BANKNOTES

These items can imply security, which may be financial but can also be emotional. Dreaming that you lose your money or jewels (or have them stolen) is a clear message of insecurity.

BLUE

▲ Van Gogh chose oppressive blue for a self-portrait painted while in an asylum.

Blue's happy associations derive from the fact that it is the color of the wide open sky—a clear sky means perspective. Blue naturally suggests infinity and transcendence. It is also the color of the ocean and may represent the ebb and flow of your emotions and moods, which can be positive or negative depending on the dream context.

POSITIVE INTERPRETATION

Bright blue—the color of a summer sky—can imply contentment and a sense of freedom, or perhaps a longing for these things. Pale blue is the traditional color associated with baby boys, so might suggest some burgeoning masculine impulse or urge. Conversely, blue is also the traditional color of the Virgin Mary and can stand for the anima (the female aspect of the unconscious), especially in an idealized form.

NEGATIVE INTERPRETATION

As a cool color, blue can be a metaphor for detachment; in spiritual matters this can be positive, but in affairs of the heart it can suggest separation or an absence of love. Darker blues can represent depression or other forms of emotional negativity.

A BLUEBIRD

This species of bird represents optimism and happiness, and reassurance that you can transcend current difficulties. But if the bird is in a cage, this implies that to achieve happiness you may have to first free yourself from something that is confining or trapping you.

BLUE FIRE OR SMOKE

Smoke is generally a metaphor for something obscuring your view, but if the smoke or the flames are blue then this may indicate spiritual transformation or some kind of purification.

BLUE FLOWERS

These are a symbol of inspiration, often creative or artistic. Bluebells, with their clusters of tiny bell-shaped flowers, could be your unconscious mind drawing your attention (ringing a bell) to the beauty present in your life.

PURPLE AND VIOLET

▲ Purple is the color of deep emotions, spirituality, power, and wealth.

Purple has long been linked to religious faith across both Eastern and Western cultures: Leonardo da Vinci believed that meditation was enhanced by praying under violet rays streaming through a stained-glass window. Purple represents universal harmony in Chinese painting and the purple amethyst is sacred in Buddhism. This color is also commonly associated with royalty—which stems from the fact that purple dyes were very rare in nature and therefore costly.

POSITIVE INTERPRETATION

The appearance of purple in a dream can suggest insight or intuition—what is colored purple will give you a clearer clue to the message. Its royal connotations mean purple signifies power and wealth; perhaps your dream reflects your feelings about an authority figure in your life or your own ability to take charge of a situation.

NEGATIVE INTERPRETATION

Purple is associated with indulgence, greed, and pomposity as well as majesty and nobility. The link with authority could also suggest something to do with the law—perhaps you feel judged or have done something that you feel deserves judgment? A washed-out purple could suggest you feel powerless. In some cultures, purple is a mourning color and this meaning may be significant to you.

PURPLE ROBES OR CLOTHING

A desire for status or a wish to appear in charge is indicated. Are those around you in the dreamscape responding to you as if you were special, or do you feel fraudulent? Your feelings in the dream are a clue as to whether your unconscious is suggesting you adopt greater humility or have greater faith in yourself.

PURPLE FLOWERS

Generally, these can be symbols of adoration or respect. If the flower is a violet, conversely, this can be a sign of modesty and gentleness, and the purple pansy is a symbol of thoughtfulness.

A PURPLE HEART

In the U.S. Army the medal known as the Purple Heart is awarded to those wounded in action. Have you sustained some emotional injury that needs to be acknowledged? Recognizing the hurt may be the first step to healing.

BLACK

▲ This whorl into a black hole was painted by a patient of Carl Jung.

Black is the color of the night sky and it is thus connected with mystery and the unknown, such as black holes. Black can also represent one's shadow side (*see Witches and Wizards, page 66*). A dream in which one confronts or faces a black animal or someone dressed in black can be a positive one about self-acceptance. In Western cultures black is the color of death, so a dream in which it appears may be about mourning and loss. This may be loss of a person or—more widely—an idea or an aspect of oneself.

POSITIVE INTERPRETATION

Black is strongly associated with elegance and sophistication. It is also a color of authority—priests, judges, and other community leaders wear black to symbolize strength and impartiality. The meaning of these characters in the dream will depend on what they are doing and your feelings toward them.

NEGATIVE INTERPRETATION

Strictly speaking, black is not a color but the absence of color. It can represent unfulfilled or lost opportunities, and it also symbolizes depression or low mood. A dream in which there is an overwhelming or frightening sense of blackness or void can point to serious issues or fears. One's mood and emotions in the dream are a useful guide to interpretation.

BLACK CATS

In most of the world, a black cat is a symbol of bad luck and, in a dream, can signal lack of control. In the United Kingdom and Japan, it has the opposite meaning, so for dreamers from these countries the appearance of a black cat could mean you feel lucky.

BLACK BIRDS

Black-feathered birds, such as ravens and crows, eat flesh and are often seen as portents of death or disaster. Is this superstition playing out in your dream? A vulture has similar connotations, but can also be about someone preying on you.

BLACKBOARDS

The traditional teaching method of a schoolroom, a blackboard is waiting for a message (that can be wiped off in an instant). If there are any words, pay close attention to them. A bare blackboard suggests an open mind.

WHITE

▲ Horses represent movement; a white horse can symbolize spiritual progress.

In the East, white represents mourning and indicates death, while in the West it symbolizes purity and innocence. In a way, white is both the beginning and the end—the color of pure untarnished potential and also the color of enlightenment or perfection. White light is also the light from the heavens, representing enlightenment or the divine.

POSITIVE INTERPRETATION

Pure white can indicate the endless possibilities that exist when something is brand new— perhaps a new start or one's hopes for the future. It represents cleanliness: White paper, clean white bedsheets, or pristine white clothing. In a spiritual sense white can suggest purification or cleansing.

NEGATIVE INTERPRETATION

Doctors wear white coats, so the color can be sterile and clinical, or bloodless. It is also the color of emptiness and may demonstrate an inability to start (staring at a blank page or slate), or suggest an unknown, a void, or a vacuum.

WHITE ROBES

These are worn by pilgrims from many religions to represent simplicity and purity. Gods and angels are traditionally depicted wearing white in many cultures. If you are wearing white in a dream this may demonstrate an urge to simplify and cleanse yourself, or it may be an outward demonstration of inward perfection.

WHITE DOVES

If this symbol of peace appears in your dream this can indicate a wish to end a conflict with another person or a group—or perhaps a conflict between two aspects of your psyche.

BLACK AND WHITE

If both black and white appear in a dream this could be about balance between opposites, as in the yin-yang symbol. Or it may suggest that your life is lacking in color (or excitement). Black-and-white can suggest the printed word and by extension knowledge; or perhaps a rigid attitude in which one sees everything in black-and-white and does not acknowledge the compromise represented by gray.

COLORS

INDEX

ACKNOWLEDGMENTS

Quantum Books would like to acknowledge the following for supplying images reproduced in this book:

Alamy Stock Photo: p.35 age fotostock; pp.51, 129 Peter Horree; p.112 Artokoloro Quint Lox Limited; p.118 AF archive

Internet Book Archive via Flickr: p.15 University of North Carolina at Chapel Hill; p.101 University of Pittsburgh Library System; p.122 Smithsonian Libraries

Library of Congress, Prints and Photographs Division: pp. 22, 25, 46, 60

Shutterstock: p.2 marina shin; p.8–9 Tithi Luadthong; p.11 Renata Sedmakova; pp.18–19 MR.LIGHTMAN1975; pp. 26, 27, 31, 53, 55, 58, 62, 63, 65, 66, 70, 76, 79, 82, 86, 90, 131 Everett Collection; p. 32 Reeed; p.56 Oleg Golovnev; pp. 24, 59, 61, 94, 102, 114, 116, 117, 126, 134, 136, 138, 141 Everett – Art; p.67 nodff; p.73 Panayot Savov; p.75 Sergey Kohi; p.77 Sasa Prudkov; p.80 Marzolino; p.81 artivo; p.83 Elena Dijour; p.84 Dina Saeed; p.89 Marzolino; p.98 Andrew Mayovskyy; p.109 DeepGreen; p.111 outdoorsman; p.127 Jorg Hackemann; p.132 Suchota; p.133 plule_r

Wellcome Library, London: pp.7, 29, 33, 36, 42, 45, 52, 57, 87, 91, 95, 97, 106, 107, 115, 119, 121, 123, 124, 139, 140

Wikimedia Commons: p.13 Ferdinand Hodler [Public domain]; p.17 Carlo Crivelli [Public domain]; p.23 Internet Archive Book Images [No restrictions]; p.28 Paul Cézanne [Public domain]; pp.34, 54 Amedeo Modigliani [Public domain]; p.37 Queensland Newspapers Pty Ltd [Public domain]; p.39 Dennis Jarvis from Halifax, Canada (France-003324 - Mona Lisa) [CC BY-SA 2.0]; p.40 kairoinfo4u [CC BY-SA 2.0]; p.41 By Zoro Mettini (Zoro Mettini) [CC BY-SA 3.0]; p.43 Pierre-Auguste Renoir [Public domain]; p.47 U.S. National Archives and Records Administration [Public domain]; p.48 Universitätsbibliothek Heidelberg [CC-BY-SA 3.0]; p.49 George Henry Mason [Public domain]; p.50 Brück & Sohn Kunstverlag Meißen (Own work) [CC0]; p.71 Unknown [Public domain]; p.74 Mary Cassatt [Public domain]; p.85 John William Waterhouse [Public domain]; p.93 Floris van Dyck [Public domain]; p.99 Harvard Art Museums/Fogg Museum, Gift of Mr. and Mrs. Frederic Haines Curtiss; p.105 Vincent van Gogh [Public domain]; p.105 August Macke [Public domain]; p.108 Pieter Brueghel the Elder [Public domain]; p.110 Katsushika Hokusai [Public domain]; p.113 Odilon Redon [Public domain]; p.135 J. M. W. Turner [Public domain]; p.137 Dante Gabriel Rossetti [Public domain];

While every effort has been made to credit contributors, Quantum Books would like to apologize should there have been any omissions or errors and would be pleased to make the appropriate correction to future editions of the book.